PERMISSION TO DREAM

HOW TO BE
RADICALLY
RESILIENT
AND HOPEFUL

CHRISTINE CAINE

ALSO BY CHRISTINE CAINE

PERMISSION TO DREAM

HOW TO BE
RADICALLY
RESILIENT
AND HOPEFUL

CHRISTINE CAINE

NELSON
BOOKS

An Imprint of Thomas Nelson

CONTENTS

INTRODUCTION

"There are some people who live in a dream world, and there are some who face reality; and then there are those who turn one into the other."

DOUGLAS H. EVERETT

I am not a dreamer by nature. That may sound strange to you, but I can literally count on one hand the number of dreams I remember having in my lifetime. Given that I have been alive for almost six decades, that means I may have had one dream I remember every ten years or so. My daughter Sophia, on the other hand, is the exact opposite. She dreams almost every night, and from what she describes, it's always in Technicolor. She can recount the most vivid and inspiring details to me. There's nothing I love more than over a breakfast of vegemite toast, Sophia telling me all about the previous night's dreams.

Even when it comes to having a life dream or plan, I was never the type of kid who had one. I never thought about what I wanted to be when I grew up. Having experienced a lot of trauma in my childhood, I was too busy trying to survive to have any energy left to dream about the future. But the good news is that even when I didn't have a dream for my life, God always did. He created me on purpose and for a purpose. As I grew closer to him in my early adult years, I discovered those dreams, and I have spent the past four decades working them into my life. I believe that all of the things I do—like rescuing the victims of human trafficking through A21, empowering women through Propel, reaching the lost, and building up the Church through Equip & Empower—are the good works God had prepared for me before I ever arrived on Earth. Paul writes in Ephesians 2:10 that "we are his workmanship created in Christ Jesus for good works, which God prepared ahead of time for us to do."

God had a dream for you and me before we ever got here, and it is my hope and prayer that through the pages of this short book you will be inspired to passionately pursue God's dream(s) for your life.

I understand that life is full of so many twists and turns, and we can become so discouraged, disappointed, or disillusioned that we start to believe the lie that our lives have no purpose or that there's no point daring to dream. I know that dreams can turn to nightmares. False starts, failed endeavors, betrayals, and losses can lead to cynicism, hopelessness, or despair. Our thoughts can take us places, can't they?

Why dream when nothing good ever happens to me?

Why dream when I never get a break?

Why dream when God seems to prefer everyone else to me?

Why dream when I'm already so far behind there's no hope my dreams could become a reality?

I am living proof that regardless of where you start in life, you can fulfill God's dream and purpose for your life. I am living proof that no matter what has been done or said to you in your past, what Jesus did for you at Calvary is greater, so you can have a life beyond your past and fulfill God's dream for your life. I am living proof that you do not need to be the best, fastest, smartest, most popular, most resourced, or most highly educated person in the room to fulfill God's dream for your life. I am living proof that you are never too young or too old to pursue God's dream for your life. I am living proof that your mistakes and failures are not final, and if you are still breathing, God still has a plan. God is able to redeem anything, restore anything, and renew your passion and purpose. In Christ, you have permission to dream, and if necessary, dream again.

Has God given you a dream? What I love about the desires and dreams God gives us is that they are always connected to our calling. Are you familiar with this word? Our calling comes with a multilayered meaning of strategic purpose, specific intent, and concrete direction. It's our assignment, our vocation. It's a purpose outside of ourselves that brings God glory and blesses others. It's how we light up our part of this world.

I know from experience that it doesn't matter if you don't think you have the courage, the strength, the wisdom, the money, the influence, the experience, the education, the organization, or the backing to fulfill your calling. If God shows you something he wants you to do, in him and with his strength, you can do it. He doesn't call the qualified. He qualifies the called.

Our callings can be as different as we are, but we are all called to do something, and ultimately that something brings glory to God. Maybe God has given you a dream to:

- become a doctor or a lawyer, mathematician or astronaut.
- be an Olympic athlete.
- write a book or screenplay.
- become a musician or actor.

- mentor young people in after-school tutoring programs.
- reach out to women in recovery programs who need to hear, "Yes, you can."
- build a network for young moms and help them launch home-based businesses.
- lead a neighborhood Bible study, providing a safe place for people to grow.
- go back to school or start a business or change careers.
- pitch in at your neighborhood's community center.

Whatever your dream is, God wants you to pursue it—and he has given you his very own Spirit to help you to become all he has created you to be and do all that he has called you to do. Furthermore, if you feel you don't have a dream right now, ask him for one. If you feel it's too late, you're too far gone, or you've made too many mistakes to ask him for a dream, I have good news for you—it's not. He's given you permission to dream again, so feel free to ask him why he has placed you on this earth at this time, in your particular location, with your specific personality, gifts, and talents. It's never too late because we are called to keep bearing fruit while we are alive on planet Earth. I'm fifty-seven right now, and no matter how much I have achieved, I know that there is still more ahead. If my race were already completed, I would be home in heaven right now. Since I'm not, and if you are reading this book, then I assume you're not either, it's time to keep dreaming and keep believing God for what he puts in our hearts to do.

Jesus prayed, "As you sent me into the world, I also have sent them into the world."[1] God has sent me, and he has sent you. He has sent us out with different dreams and callings, but every single one of them is designed to include reaching people. Loving them. Encouraging them. Serving them. I can't wait to share with you—through my stories and those of a few friends—why I know you can do everything he's put in your heart to do—even if you aren't sure what all that is yet!

Love,

Chris Carè

1

SEE WHAT GOD SEES AND
LOOK TO YOUR FUTURE

*Healing takes courage, and we
all have courage, even if we
have to dig a little to find it.*
TORI AMOS

I didn't exactly have a good start when I came into this world, but how we start doesn't have to determine how we finish—especially when God gets involved and drops dreams into our hearts that he wants us to fulfill. Because my life is living proof of this, it is important to me that I share part of my story with you. My life shows what God can do in a person's life when we invite him in to help us be all he created us to be and to do all that he's called us to do.

When I was born, from all the research I've conducted and professionals I've spoken to, my birth mother was young, unmarried, and pregnant in a time when young women like her would have been ostracized, rejected, and possibly have nowhere to go but a home for unwed mothers where conditions were often deplorable. She would have had no means of providing for me, as my father was not in the picture at the time of my birth. His name is noticeably absent from my birth certificate. According to hospital records, my mother entered the hospital alone, gave birth alone, and left as soon as she could. And as one professional once said to me, she had to have been vulnerable and most likely taken advantage of, much like the women I help rescue today through the work of A21.

For the following two weeks after I was born, I was left in the hospital, unnamed and unwanted. My birth certificate merely lists me as Number 2,508 of 1966. At the end of two weeks, I was adopted by a family of like ethnicity, as that's how things were done back then. If you were a Greek baby, they matched you up with a Greek family. The Greek family that adopted me loved me dearly, and for that I will always be grateful.

But growing up Greek in Australia in the late

1960s and early 1970s wasn't easy culturally. I grew up being marginalized because of my ethnicity, gender, and socioeconomic background. I actually lived in the poorest zip code at the time in Sydney. Every day as I walked to elementary school and then high school, I walked past graffiti that labeled us and told us to go home, though home was Sydney. Daily, I was the subject of racial slurs and the bullying that just went with being Greek in our community.

Furthermore, and I don't share this lightly, I was also sexually abused as a child for many years. Men I trusted—men my parents trusted—betrayed our trust and my innocence. The *Oxford English Dictionary* defines *abuse* as "using an object for a purpose other than that for which it was designed." For many years, unbeknownst to my parents, I was used for a purpose for which I was never designed. Let me tell you, that messes with you big-time.

Though I didn't learn that I was adopted until

I was thirty-three, all these experiences were traumatic and left lasting effects that took me years to process. The pain seeped into every crevice of my heart, affecting how I developed mentally, emotionally, and relationally; it formed me in so many ways and informed my decisions along the way. It was only through my relationship with Jesus and the work of the Holy Spirit, along with professional help and therapy, and a lot of internal work, that I found a life beyond my past. It was in God that I found I didn't have to let my history define my destiny, that what Jesus did for me was greater than what anyone had done to me and could do to me. I'm so grateful that what happened to me in my past didn't stop God from using me. In fact, his determination to heal me and use me was unstoppable. Despite all I'd been through, he still dropped dreams in my heart of things he wanted me to do. Oftentimes, I think he used me not in spite of my past, but because of my past. My life's verse says it best: "You intended to harm me, but God intended it for good to accomplish what is now being done, the saving of many lives."[1]

I understand the reality that nothing I say or do will change the things that were done to me. The past is set and can't be changed. What happened happened. But to this day, I can make choices that will determine my future. We all can. By putting God at the center of our lives, by dealing with the issues that hold us back, and by recognizing that the plans of God for our future are bigger than the pain and regret of our past, we can get up from wherever we are at this moment and move forward. We can live out the dreams he gives us.

I have no idea what life has thrown your way, but regardless of what it is and how bad it might be, I want to see you thrive. I want to see you flourish and fulfill your purpose. And I know from experience it's possible. I am so grateful I found a way to reconcile my past in Christ and move forward into the future he has for me. Looking back, my decision impacted not only me, but also everyone around me, including generations coming after me.

Cleaning out and renovating our internal world requires an ongoing, focused commitment on our part. Though I've come a long way, I'm still learning and relearning through the work of Christ that's ongoing in me. It has taken me years of hard work and persistent prayer to move through the pain and wounds of my past and to keep growing through them. I've needed to repeatedly return to the throne of grace and seek God's strength to forgive and grow. That's how the work of transformation is: it takes time and diligent effort.

What good news, then, that this ongoing work in us doesn't stop us from running our race, as Paul called it, doing all that God's called us to do.

"Don't you know that the runners in a stadium all race, but only one receives the prize? Run in such a way to win the prize."[2]

As we run our race here on Earth, we receive God's on-the-job training in Christlikeness. The book of Hebrews tells us that we aren't required, under our own strength, to throw off what hinders us in order to take part in the race.[3] Instead, we are invited to throw it all off *as we run*.

If we want to be unstoppable in our race, then we need to constantly challenge ourselves to keep cleaning out the internal world of our hearts and minds so that we continue to have more room to contain more of the power of God within us. Remember, as Christ in us grows larger, our old selves grow smaller. Unloading all the baggage of our past makes a lot of room for Christ in us to grow.

I don't know what your past is. I don't know what pains or sorrows or wounds you carry. But I do know that God can turn all of it around and then use your past to give someone else a future. That's what Jesus does. In every way we are healed, in every way we grow in Christ, we're to pass that on. We're to pass on our faith and life experiences from one person to another, from one generation to the next. This is what happens when we answer his call, when we hear him say, "Follow me," and respond in obedience.

MEET FAVOUR

I want to tell you a story that illustrates this so well. It's about a woman named Favour who was trafficked, rescued through the work of A21, and went through the aftercare program of A21 to lead a new and independent life. She invited God into her life, to heal her, to give her new dreams, to go on and pursue all his plans and purposes for her life. She inspires me to this day because she's still pursuing him.

Favour's story began when her cousin tricked her into moving to Greece for a job and used a witch doctor to control and manipulate her.

"When you get to Greece, you will do whatever your cousin tells you to do," the witch doctor said.

And Favour, kneeling before the witch doctor, repeated, "When I get to Greece, I will do whatever my cousin tells me to do."

"You will not speak to strangers."

"I will not speak to strangers."

"You will not tell anyone who took you to Greece."

"I will not tell anyone who took me to Greece."

"And if you do, you will die or go mad."

Shocked, Favour gasped. Those words she could not bring herself to repeat. And why was she having to repeat any words a witch doctor prompted her to say?

Favour was brought up by her father and stepmother in Nigeria, because her mother deserted her when she was two years old. And not only did her father and stepmother treat her badly, they also raised her to believe in the false power of a witch doctor.

For Favour it was miserable. "When I was sixteen, my dad told me to leave his house and find somewhere else to stay." So, for the next two years, Favour lived with a married couple and their five children in a small apartment, working as a housemaid—and fending off the husband's sexual harassment and advances. When she was eighteen, a cousin invited Favour to come live with her in Greece. "I accepted because I needed money to study to become a nurse. I have a passion to care for people and give them hope. I was excited!"

But then the cousin told her that before she left Nigeria, she would need to see a witch doctor. "I was so scared! When he asked me to say that I would die or go mad if I broke my oath, I refused. But then they told me that if I did not say the words, I would not leave the witch doctor's house alive, and I believed them. I had heard bad stories about witch doctors, about how they kill people and have the power to make someone go mad. So

I repeated his words; I said the oath. And then he made me say that if I even told anyone about the oath, I would die. I believed that it was true."

HELD CAPTIVE BY THE ENEMY

In my years in ministry, I've been honored to witness God's power at work in the lives of many women, including former trafficking victims. Favour is one of those women. With a story that begins so shrouded in darkness and deceit, it's always astounding to see God's light pierce such darkness and his truth overcome such deception.

The events of Favour's life bring into sharp focus that she had natural enemies, which were her traffickers, and she faced the unavoidable reality that we all have a spiritual enemy. If we run our race well, he has so much to lose, so he's not an enemy to be taken lightly.

As we progress in running our race, we

naturally go through times of receiving, releasing, multiplying, and growing. And the whole time, as the Enemy sees us faithfully and consistently moving through these God-ordained times; he knows his territory is threatened. Therefore, he plots and schemes to thwart us in our run, to trip us up, to stop us in our tracks. For this reason, we must be alert and throw off any weights that would slow us down or give him a weapon to use against us.

Favour's story is especially meaningful to me, not only because we see her move from the captivity of her traffickers' deceit to a life of physical freedom to thriving as an independent person, but also because her story inspires us all to find the courage to throw off whatever hinders us in our own race.

FREEDOM FOR FAVOUR

Despite the frightening oath that Favour was forced to take before leaving her home country, she was excited to go. After all, her cousin had been like a sister to her before moving to Greece. But soon after Favour arrived, she had her first disturbing shock: Favour's cousin had another woman physically beat her, for no apparent reason at all. After the beating, Favour's cousin revealed the promised job: Favour would work as a prostitute.

"I told her I could not do it. I could not sleep with men. But she told me that this was the only way to pay her back the money she used to bring me to Greece—60,000 euros. I had no choice. I had taken an oath that whatever she told me to do, I would do. I was terrified! I saw no way out. I didn't know anyone and didn't want to die from breaking the oath. And I knew that if I didn't do what she wanted, she would beat me.

"Every day was like living in hell. Sometimes I had to service forty or fifty men a day. There were times when I wanted to commit suicide. When I got home, my cousin would take all the money from me. 'Remember the oath,' she would say, 'or you will go mad or die.'"

Favour survived two years of this—two years of praying that God would get her out of her living hell—until one day, at the medical clinic where prostitutes were required by Greek law to report to be checked for diseases, she came in contact with a woman who knew about the work of A21.

Hearing the woman speak and recognizing the accent as familiar, Favour asked the woman where she was from. When the woman told her that she was from South Africa, Favour said quietly, "Speak English, then—the madam doesn't understand it." The madam from the brothel always accompanied the girls to the clinic, so she wasn't far away.

The two women spoke in English, and every now and then one of them would say something silly, and they would laugh as if they were just chatting. But actually, the woman was asking Favour for her story, and when she found that Favour was being trafficked, she asked Favour why she didn't go to the police. "They told me that if I go to the police," Favour said, "they will tell their associates in Nigeria, who will kill my family."

The two women began to meet secretly before or after Favour's shift at the brothel. During that same time, though Favour didn't know much about the Christian faith, one night as she was alone in her bedroom, she prayed to accept Jesus.

Not long after that night, the police, after months of investigation, conducted a raid on Favour's cousin's home and arrested everyone living there—the cousin, the cousin's boyfriend, and Favour. They were taken to the police station, and the woman privately met with Favour there.

"I was very scared in the beginning," Favour said. "I was afraid that if my cousin learned that I had been talking to someone, and that was why we had been arrested, I would be beaten or even killed, as most girls are who speak out or try to escape. But the woman told me she knew of an organization that would help me through it all."

When Favour was brought to the A21 safe house, she met other girls who had been in the same situation. Our team gave her a room to sleep in and food to eat. Soon, Favour was experiencing love and care as she never had before in her life.

When the date for the trial of her traffickers came, Favour was so afraid of facing them again, particularly her cousin, that when she got to the courthouse, she was shaking. The trial lasted two days. Favour said, "When the lawyers called and told us that the traffickers had been sentenced to four years in jail, I jumped up and down for joy. A weight had been lifted off my shoulders. I could live again!"

That day, upon hearing of the traffickers' convictions, Favour realized more than ever that she did not belong to her sex traffickers, but to Jesus. And though she was free physically, she discovered that there was more to becoming free than escaping a brothel. She'd suffered all her life—first abandoned as a child and a teen, then harassed by her employer, then forced into hopeless degradation as a sex worker. With help that comes from counseling, Favour recognized the anger, bitterness, and emotional scars she carried. She'd spent years contending with nightmares and fears, shame and guilt, feelings of worthlessness and hopelessness. She came to realize that she had to shed those hindrances that kept her entangled in the emotions and attitudes of her old life. And a huge part of that was learning to forgive, but Favour's lesson in forgiveness didn't come easily—or quickly.

"The ones I found it hardest to forgive were my father, because he drove me away from home; my stepmother, because she treated me badly; and my cousin, because she lied to me and made me sleep with men for money. Those things hurt me badly, and forgiving those three took me a very long time."

A very long time. Favour's simple words compress a lot of pain and struggle into a small space. For her, as for us all, forgiveness was . . . complicated. In many ways, it was like recovering from a horror movie in which she'd played the lead. First, she had to heal physically from the considerable damage she'd experienced in her body. Then she had to heal mentally and emotionally—no small task for any victim of trafficking. So much of what she had to process extended to her earliest memories.

And yet, the same God who is accessible to you and me healed Favour's heart. As she did the hard work internally, and as she grew to know God better, Favour invited God to become bigger in her life than the injustices she'd suffered, than the wounds inflicted upon her body and psyche, than the horror and pain of her past. And because she did, she was able to throw off those things that hindered her and step into the "exceedingly abundantly above"[4] future that God had prepared for her before the foundation of the world. And she followed God's leading into a dream she long held . . . to further her education. With the help of A21, she graduated college, and as she so aptly said, "All my life is new."

That same hope exists for us all, no matter how impossible our dreams might seem.

CHOICES

Like each of us, Favour faced a choice: she could have surrendered to the temptation to harbor the hate and resentment against those who made her life hellish for years, or do the hard work necessary to forgive and to heal. Who would have more right to harbor unforgiveness than a woman like Favour who had been forced to live a life of degradation, brutality, and humiliation? Still, she made the choice that would move her life forward. If Favour, so young in her faith and so betrayed by life, can find the wherewithal to cast aside, to throw off, the entanglements that would hinder God's work in her life, then consider the hope that you can do the same.

What are some of those things that hinder and entangle? That can hold us back from God's plans and purposes for us? Here are just a few examples:

- Unforgiveness
- Bitterness
- Shame
- Rejection
- Offense
- Lust
- Greed
- Envy
- Deceit
- Insecurity
- Fear
- Doubt
- Indifference

- Apathy
- False belief systems

Do any of those things sound familiar? Does it sound like I took that list right from your own life?

I didn't. I took it from mine.

Our dreams come from God. He is using us, not in spite of our past, but because of our past. With his help, we have the ability to get up wherever we are, no matter what, and move forward. We have the power to walk in everything he's called us to do.

WHAT YOU'VE LEARNED

* We can't change what has happened to us, but we can choose to move forward toward Jesus.

* Sometimes, God uses us not in spite of our pasts but because of our pasts.

* We must throw off anything that hinders us in our race.

QUESTIONS FOR REFLECTION

Can you relate to Favour's story or her feelings? Which parts?

....

....

....

....

....

....

....

How do you define forgiveness? Must it always involve a conversation with the person who wronged you, or can it be an internal process? Is there anyone you need to forgive?

What is keeping you from running the race set before you? Take a moment to name the things holding you back.

2

ACKNOWLEDGE YOUR FUTURE AND REMOVE THE SHAME

Loss is the uninvited door that extends us an unexpected invitation to unimaginable possibilities.
CRAIG D. JONESBOROUGH

We all have things we need to remove from our lives in order to keep moving forward fulfilling all the plans and purposes God has for our lives. In fact, we need to regularly take inventory, because it's surprising how quickly the things we once removed can come back and cling to us again.

Take a moment right now to pause and ask yourself, "What do I need to remove in order to run my race well?" The list could include any number of things. What about unresolved anger that is hurting your relationships, causing you to say things you later regret? Perhaps you are carrying resentment or selfishness or pride. Or a lack of confidence and a spirit of defeat that hinder your ability to make wise choices. Or a lack of financial planning and discipline that hamper your ability to be generous with your resources, even though you would love to be. Or you may have unresolved issues from the past that are harming your parenting skills. Does insecurity about your abilities or looks cause you to be judgmental and critical of others?

Are you tethered to destructive friends, unhealthy lifestyles, or negative habits? Are you too overly enamored with financial gain, career success, or plentiful leisure time to the point that they hold you back from giving the time and energy necessary to run the race God has called you to run?

Whatever it is that holds you back, you can get rid of it by the power of the Holy Spirit. It may take some time, but don't let these things hinder you from your dreams and your purpose. Too much is at stake to let them hold you back. You really can live free from your past mistakes, hurts, and misconceptions. I understand that old habits die hard. Breaking our comfortable, familiar patterns takes work. Hard work. But if we don't break from our past, then we'll never run toward our new future.

God promises us, "'For I know the plans I have for you'—this is the LORD's declaration—'plans for your well-being, not for disaster, to give you a future and a hope.'"[1]

Here is the simple truth: we cannot go where we are going without leaving where we have been. So ask yourself, "What must I leave behind in order to run my race and serve God with my whole life?" God is looking for runners who, like Paul, will say:

> But everything that was a gain to me, I have considered to be a loss because of Christ. More than that, I also consider everything to be a loss in view of the surpassing value of knowing Christ Jesus my Lord. Because of him I have suffered the loss of all things and consider them as dung, so that I may gain Christ.[2]

Imagine the freedom that will come when you are willing to work through whatever it is that you need to work through so you can exchange it all for the surpassing greatness of becoming an unstoppable runner in the work God calls you to do. Anticipate the joy of moving forward into the future he has for you. Make a defining decision of unhindered commitment to Jesus Christ and his cause and step out in faith.

Do you want God to do something new in your life? Has God given you a dream to pursue? Then you will need to take the steps necessary to stop doing the same old thing. Ask God to help you. He's always for you.

Do you want God to change your circumstances? Then be willing to change even in the face of feeling uncomfortable. To be honest, change is rarely easy, but when it's something God wants us to change, it's always worth it.

One thing I do: Forgetting what is behind and straining toward what is ahead, I press on toward the goal to win the prize for which

God has called me heavenward in Christ Jesus.[3]

YOU CAN CHANGE THE FUTURE

Once you've removed what you should not be holding on to, you are free to grasp the dreams and assignments related to your calling. I know from experience that you cannot be grabbing what's ahead if you're holding on to what's behind. Your capacity to grab what's next is determined by how wide you open your hands as you await what God has in store for you.

When you are living for the race, you'll be running that race all week long, all month long, all year long, and all life long, actively and passionately seeking where God is at work and joining him in that work. You'll be intentionally and purposefully pursuing your dreams and carrying your calling into the building where you work, into your interactions with your neighbors, into your community, your school, your grocery store, your bank, even your own home, always on the lookout for what God wants to accomplish through you in every circumstance.

Just consider the power of carrying your calling into those places rather than dragging along the ball and chain of hurts and resentments, sins and scars, and old priorities that are not God's priorities. You will feel lighter and run as a beacon of light for God's glory rather than hibernating in a dark den surrounded by the weights of the past. Such freedom awaits you as you remove those things that hinder you from becoming an unstoppable runner in God's divine race.

Are you ready to put an end to all that holds you back, so you can run like the wind into everything God has planned for you? Then do so. Put an end to being held back. Endings, it turns out, are the perfect place for a new start.

God promises that the plans he has for you are for good and not for evil, to give you a future and a hope.[4] Instead of choosing to live weighed down by the past when his promises are beckoning you into your future, cut yourself free from all that hinders and cast it all away so you can experience the truth of Psalm 40:1–3:

> I waited patiently for the LORD,
>   and he turned to me and heard my
>   cry for help.
> He brought me up from a
>   desolate pit,
>   out of the muddy clay,
> and set my feet on a rock,
>   making my steps secure.
> He put a new song in my mouth,
>   a hymn of praise to our God.
> Many will see and fear,
>   and they will trust in the LORD.

STEPS TOWARD WHOLENESS AND HEALING

It's hard for someone who is supposed to have it all together to admit that she needs help. But that's exactly what I had to do. Hurting people hurt other people. When Nick and I were dating, I was hurting, and because of that, I hurt him and who knows how many others. If I were to stop hurting and instead find wholeness and healing, then I needed to forgive those who had abused me. But I also needed to go further: I needed to trust Nick, who loved me, and I needed healing in my relationship with God.

I grappled with this idea for weeks after Nick and I had a long talk where I told him all about my past. At the time, I also was teaching students how to trust God in their daily walk, and now I had to learn to do that myself at a whole new level.

I had so many questions, and my questions

were so big that I took them to a counselor. Though the walls around my heart had been pounded, they were still standing. I would never be free from the haunting memories and old feelings of shame, self-condemnation, anger, bitterness, and mistrust until I determined to make new memories and embrace new feelings such as peace, kindness, and compassion.

The process of breaking free and walking in wholeness starts within. The healing process ahead of me would take the touch of God's hand, as well as deliberation and work—and no elixir I could sip nor pill I could pop would take away that process or its pain.

Healing, for any of us, doesn't happen overnight, but it does happen. If we trust God with our broken and wounded hearts, then he will bring healing, restoration, and wholeness. He takes the weak, the marginalized, and the oppressed and makes all things new. What someone else would leave for broken, he sees as beautiful. He sees us beyond where we are; he sees us as who he created us to be. That's the pattern of God I see in his Word. It's the pattern I see in the story of the lame man who was begging at the temple gate. People had walked by him for years, giving him money or ignoring him, but when Peter and John walked by, God reached out to him, just like he was reaching out to me.

"Now Peter and John were going up to the temple for the time of prayer at three in the afternoon. A man who was lame from birth was being carried there. He was placed each day at the temple gate called Beautiful, so that he could beg from those entering the temple. When he saw Peter and John about to enter the temple, he asked for money. Peter, along with John, looked straight at him and said, "Look at us." So he turned to them, expecting to get something from them. But Peter said, "I don't have silver or gold, but what I do have, I give you: In the name of Jesus Christ of Nazareth, get up and walk!" Then, taking him by the right hand he raised him up, and at once his feet and ankles became strong. So he jumped up and started to walk, and he entered the temple with them—walking, leaping, and praising God. All the people saw him walking and praising God, and they recognized that he was the one who used to sit and beg at the Beautiful Gate of the temple. So they were filled with awe and astonishment at what had happened to him.[5]

The man who was begging had been lame from birth. When other babies were taking their first steps, he did not. When other kids were running and playing, he could not. When teenagers were working alongside their parents, learning a trade, he could not. His muscles would have been atrophied, his limbs shriveled, distorted. Much like our souls are from the time we're wounded.

We know from this passage that he was dependent on others to carry him from his home to the temple area, up fifteen steps to the gate, and place him there in front of it. He was laid daily at the temple gate. The routine was set, the plan was set, the system was set, and everyone acted according to the expectation. When we expect and accept that this is how things will always be, we build our lives around daily rituals that enable and ensure the life we have settled for.

Because of his condition, he was not allowed to enter beyond the gate. He was ostracized, marginalized, discarded, and overlooked. He was someone society would have seen as ugly and labeled undesirable. The people entering the temple to pray at three in the afternoon would have noticed him—every single day.

God chose to put the story of someone like this—someone who physically wasn't easy to look at—in his inspired and holy Word, and the story took place in front of a gate called Beautiful. What irony.

That gate was one of a kind. Unlike all the other gates around the temple, which were plated in gold and silver, this one was made of solid, brilliant Corinthian brass.[6] It was magnificent and massive, an unusual size of more than sixty feet wide, more than thirty feet tall.[7] Its weight was so great that it took twenty men to move it. It gleamed in the afternoon sun, outshining all the others. It was strategically placed between two courts. The first court, where everyone entered, was inside the wall surrounding the temple—the holy ground of the outer court. On the other side of the gate called Beautiful was the inner court—the place of prayer and worship, the place of the presence of God.

The lame man was doomed to stay there, sitting outside against the massive doors of the gate, sentenced to a life of brokenness, until Peter and John came along. Until God extended to him an invitation.

The lame man asked for money.

Peter responded, "Look at us." He sought to dignify, value, and humanize this man by asking him to look at them.

And the man had the courage to look at them, to look up. To change his perspective from being low to the ground, staring at his misery, to looking heavenward, where healing and miracles come from.

"I don't have silver or gold," Peter said, "but what I do have, I give you: In the name of Jesus Christ of Nazareth, walk."

I love this story because it shows that we often overestimate what people can do for us and underestimate what God wants to do for us. The man asked for money. Peter offered him healing. The man wanted a short-term solution. Peter offered him what he really needed—not pocket change but a life change.

Isn't that like God? To take what is ugly and make it beautiful? To reach out to us right where we are, where we seemingly don't fit in, and heal us? To see beyond our brokenness to all the potential he placed inside us?

When Peter told the lame man to get up and walk, the man obeyed. He made the effort to rise up. To move forward in faith. That's all God ever asks us to do.

"Then, taking him by the right hand he raised him up, and at once his feet and ankles became strong. So he jumped up and started to walk."

Then he stepped foot where he'd never been able to go before. "He entered the temple with them—walking, leaping, and praising God."

God cherishes us in our brokenness, but he'll never leave us there. He sends people—like Peter and John, like Nick—to notice us and show us his unconditional love. And then, as he heals us, he uses us to touch others: "All the people saw him walking and praising God, and they recognized that he was the one who used to sit and beg at the Beautiful Gate of the temple. So they were filled with awe and astonishment at what had happened to him."

When the people saw the man and recognized him, a crowd gathered. It became the perfect opportunity for Peter to preach, and the man was used as a witness to the power and person of Jesus.[8]

Our healing is always for more than just us. It's for all the people on the other side of our obedience. When the man looked up, he obeyed, undeterred, and he was healed. The result: multitudes came to Christ.

Isn't this the same work God was doing in me? Isn't this what he wants to do in you? He wants to lead us all through the gate called Beautiful, right into his presence. To put us on the path to our destiny, to living out all the dreams he's given us, to fulfilling our calling—so multitudes can be helped.

WHAT YOU'VE LEARNED

* If we want God to do something new in our lives, we need to take the steps necessary to stop doing the same old thing.

* The process of breaking free and walking in wholeness starts within.

* All God ever asks us to do is to move forward in faith.

QUESTIONS FOR REFLECTION

What must you leave behind in order to serve God with your whole life?

....

....

....

....

....

....

....

Has there been a time in your life where you've overestimated what people can do for you and underestimated what God wants to do for you?

....

....

....

....

....

....

....

....

....

Who has God placed in your life to show you his unconditional love? How can you show this love to others?

_____

_____

_____

_____

_____

_____

_____

_____

_____

_____

_____

3

ACCEPTING DISAPPOINTMENT

AND REMAINING HOPEFUL

*We must accept finite
disappointment, but never
lose infinite hope.*
—MARTIN LUTHER KING, JR.

W hen I first met my friend LoriAnn, I never would have guessed the heartache she had lived through. I was hosting an A21 awareness trip in Thessaloniki, Greece, for a group of women from her church, and over a lunch of Greek salad with extra feta cheese, we clicked. She is Lebanese and Syrian, and with me being Greek, we joked that maybe it was because of our Mediterranean blood. It was fun to meet a woman who could talk as fast as me, was as passionate, driven, and focused as me, and gestured with her hands as much as I did.

One evening, at a tiny Greek restaurant, our dinner transitioned into a late-night conversation about everything, including all the loss she had endured and the dream that had died.

"You can get dressed now, LoriAnn."

Covered only by a light blanket and sheet, LoriAnn stirred slightly at the sound of the nurse's voice. Still foggy-headed from the waning sedative, she felt helpless to move, much less get up. The heaviness of her heart and all the years of struggle seemed to weigh her down, pinning her to the bed. Squinting against the harsh fluorescent lights, straining to focus, she tried to will her body into action, but all she could manage was to grasp the outer edge of the blanket.

Glancing at her surroundings, she noticed the curtain had been pulled aside, exposing the rest of the recovery room. It appeared as sterile and disappointing as her last sonogram. Where there should have been a bright, pulsing miracle of life, there had been only stillness. Instinctively, her hand went to her abdomen. The place her growing baby had been was now just a knot of grief and anxiety. She had loved him from the moment he was hoped for through all the time she carried him. Her heart had never quit beating for him—even when his gave out. She would never stop loving him. Never stop wanting to hold him.

"You can get up and get dressed when you're ready," the nurse repeated.

The groggy effects of the anesthesia were wearing off, but what remained pushed LoriAnn to a jagged edge.

And then what? Go home and pretend nothing ever happened? Go back to work and try to act like everything's normal? Nothing is normal. And nothing will ever be normal again. All I wanted was a baby . . . my baby.

The nurse simply meant it as a kind prompt, but LoriAnn's frayed mind couldn't stop intensifying her broken heart and the harsh betrayal of her empty womb.

You can get dressed now because:
You will never be a mother.
You will never celebrate Mother's Day.

You are flawed. Broken. Ill-equipped. Irreparable. And there's nothing you can do about any of it.

Rolling to her side and burying her face in the sheet, LoriAnn wanted to cry, wanted to feel the release, but she couldn't. The flare of anger had collapsed into feelings of nothingness and numbness—the calm that always preceded the storm she knew would come. She knew getting dressed wouldn't help anything. It wouldn't erase years of fading hopes. It wouldn't quench the longing in her soul. It wouldn't prepare her for the silence waiting at home. That's where the tears would come—in the profound sadness and loneliness waiting for her in the echoing quiet of her bedroom. No clothes would ever hide her shattered heart or cover all the shame she felt. Nothing was going to shield her from the insensitive things people would say, even if they meant well, especially when they offered, "Don't worry, you can always try again," or "Well, it's not like losing an actual child."

Yes, it was. It was exactly like losing my *child.*

Too many times, those kinds of comments had seared her heart and left her doubled over inside. She had always managed to mumble some niceties, but this time, she knew she could never bear it again—because she could never try again. She had fought so hard to stay pregnant—every time she had been pregnant—but this time marked the end of a battle she no longer had the strength to fight. A battle that left her no choice but to surrender.

She knew the tsunami of emotions would come—as they had each time before. The grief that would evolve into rage, relentlessly crashing into her every waking thought and sleep-deprived dreams. The edge she would topple over every time she overheard women complain about being pregnant or about their children. The bitterness and resentment that would take up long-term occupancy in her heart and become so hard to evict.

It was so unfair. All she had ever wanted to be was a mother. From the time she played with dolls as a child to when she babysat as a teen, she imagined what it would be like to chase her own children throughout the house. The older she grew, whenever someone offered to let her hold a baby, she was already reaching for it, delighted to coo and cuddle. She found so much joy in hosting baby showers for her girlfriends, celebrating each of their newfound joys. When she married, she couldn't wait for the day when she would hold one of her own. It was just a matter of time.

But it never occurred to her that time wouldn't be able to give her what she wanted most.

Having a baby was the one thing LoriAnn had thought every woman could do—and what she'd always believed God intended for her to do. When pregnancy after pregnancy failed, she began to pray like Sarah, like Hannah, like Elizabeth, like every woman called "barren" in the Bible. And even when she tried all the modern medical efforts those women never were afforded, she found herself in the same familiar place: letting go of what she wanted to hold onto the most.

I tried, LoriAnn silently screamed. *I tried so hard.*

Nothing was as she had envisioned it to be, as she had prayed it would be, as she had hoped it would be. And nothing could silence the never-ending cry of her heart for a child. The cycle of pregnancies unexpectedly ending in miscarriage after miscarriage had taken its toll. Her emotions and her marriage had worn thin, too thin. And now, hopelessness consumed her.

WHEN DREAMS DIE

Getting up and getting dressed that day began one of the hardest uphill climbs of LoriAnn's life, because that day left her grieving the future she would never have. That day left her feeling what we all can experience when our greatest hopes and biggest dreams die—when our lives are unexpectedly interrupted with a finality we couldn't have predicted or controlled. Whether our dream was wrapped up in a baby we wanted so badly, a marriage that ended abruptly, a business venture that failed, a friendship that unraveled, a ministry that never flourished, or a job opportunity that fell through, in those shattered moments we can feel so forsaken and alone, helpless and held captive by despair. Feelings of hopelessness can leave us wanting to pull back and rewrite the rest of our lives as a smaller, safer story than the adventurous one God originally planned for us. It's so easy to grow afraid to dream again and to hope again—especially in the area of our greatest disappointment.

I remember when she finished telling her story, I sat there stunned. There was such pain in her eyes as she told me about finally accepting that the baby she had wanted most in her life could never be delivered into her arms. I recognized in her the same agonizing look I had seen before in the eyes of so many women—women who were desperate to have a child, who tried every possible procedure to do so. I couldn't imagine the hopelessness LoriAnn had known, living through such a cycle of suffering and spending more than a decade desperately trying to carry a child to term. But here she was, somehow having found a way to trust God again after all her hope had been lost. I was captivated by her faith, and I wanted to know more.

Following the loss of her last pregnancy, when she realized she could never try again, she spent the next five years battling severe and unexpected health issues that required numerous surgeries, followed by painful recoveries. And yet, even in the midst of her health challenges, she managed to advance to the top of her corporation, eventually occupying an office in Manhattan. When she was seemingly on top of the world professionally, the industry she had mastered began to crumble under an investigation by the attorney general. The fallout damaged major companies around the world, and LoriAnn was soon saying painful goodbyes to many colleagues who, through no fault of their own, had lost their jobs.

When it seemed she couldn't—and shouldn't—lose any more, she lost the one person she had trusted more than anyone. What had worn thin in her marriage finally snapped. Although she and her husband had enjoyed a strong partnership early on, all the losses over the years left deep scars on their relationship. Even the best of marriages can be broken when the volley of unexpected blows leaves no space or time to fully recover from each loss—and when one partner chooses to walk away from what both once valued and leaves no room for God to intervene or help the couple reconcile.

The month their marriage ended turned into the most devastating month of LoriAnn's life. The day her divorce was final, one of her best friends unexpectedly died. Two weeks later, her dad, the rock of her life, also passed away.

If ever there was someone who had good reason to give in to hopelessness and to give up on God, it was LoriAnn. Her life had literally unraveled—through miscarriages, health challenges, professional losses, divorce, and death. And yet here she was full of faith, having traveled to the other side of the world because she wanted to share in the work of the gospel, in a work that literally rescues exploited men, women, and children and gives them hope.

I knew from her story that it hadn't been easy to pull through the dark times. She told me how she had always been analytical, a planner, a list maker, and yet none of her preparations could stop any of the tragedies that happened one right after the other. At one point, after so much loss, she admitted she had felt resentment toward God. In her Christian walk, she had done all the right things, said all the right things, and participated in all the right things, and yet she still felt distant from God.

But that's when she chose to lean into him rather than walk away. As she drew near to him, he drew near to her.[1] I was so moved when she told me, "I knew that my God was a God of hope and a God of destiny. I knew enough to know that I could not let hopelessness be what destroyed me. I could not let my heart spiral out of control. I had to press in and trust him."

LoriAnn's description of her journey deeply resonated with what I knew to be true, that even the most hopeless situations do not have to be the end of everything. The end of a chapter—no matter how unexpected or tragic—doesn't have to be the end of our story. When all we feel is utter hopelessness, by faith we can still choose to believe that Jesus is the way, the truth, and the life—for us and for our family.[2] We can believe that Jesus has the power to recreate and redeem our lives no matter how much the destroyer has destroyed.

By faith, we can lean into Jesus and risk hoping again, trusting that he will take us by the hand and lift us up, that our lives of ruin will be made whole, that our sorrows will be comforted.[3] By faith, we can trust him to give us new dreams to dream.

Sitting before me, LoriAnn struck me as a living example of words the prophet Zechariah had used thousands of years ago when he called the Israelites "prisoners of hope."[4] Instead of living in despair for the rest of her life—living but not really living, which would have been so easy to do—she had risked it all to hope again.

CHOOSE LOCKDOWN

From a psychological perspective, and according to research by Dr. Rick Snyder (1944–2006), a professor of clinical psychology who studied hope for thirty-four years at the University of Kansas,[5] hopeful thinkers achieve more and are more successful. They are physically and psychologically healthier than less hopeful people. Snyder's hope theory, according to one summary, "defines hope as a dynamic motivational experience that is interactively derived from two distinct types of cognitive tools in the context of goal achievement—namely, pathways and agency thinking. His theory proposes that hope results from an individual's perceived ability to develop numerous and flexible pathways toward their goals, allowing them to identify barriers and strategies to overcome these as they move toward goal achievement."[6]

For example, if we were to apply Snyder's hope theory to our lives, it would be a three-step process that looks like this:

Step 1: Encourage Goal-Oriented Thinking

Goals can be long-term or short-term. Be intentional and set your goals. What goals do you need to achieve to answer your calling? What dreams are you wanting to make a reality?

Step 2: Find Pathways to Achievement

A pathway is a workable route to your goals. If a setback occurs, be creative, and find another pathway. It's not going to be easy, but identifying the barriers, complications, or risks will allow you to problem-solve and create a plan.

Step 3: Instigate Change

Take time to develop good habits that will allow you to keep moving forward and in the direction of achieving your goals. Be flexible and willing to create new pathways. Be open to change and allow it to fuel your motivation.

Snyder says hope is the state of mind that helps you navigate life's twists and turns, and keeps you moving forward when times are tough. What's more, as we shall see, hope isn't simply a happy feeling—it's a human survival mechanism that fuels your desire to keep pushing on and growing.[7]

To me, from my own experiences and walk of faith with God, hope is unshakeable confidence in God.[8] It doesn't deny the reality of our pain, but it does give us a life beyond our pain. It gives us permission to believe in a new beginning. It gives us permission to dream again. It is the happy and confident expectation of good that lifts our spirits and dares us to believe in a different future—in a different dream. It is always looking to God with expectation: "Now, Lord, what do I wait for? My hope is in you."[9]

But when we lose hope, when all we feel is the pain of loss and disappointment, it can be so hard to believe that God wants to help us or that he cares, because we have more questions than answers. More doubt than faith. And yet, that is the perfect time to become a prisoner of hope.

A prisoner of hope sounds like an odd thing to be, doesn't it? Aren't prisoners locked up in high-security institutions and stripped of all their freedoms? Why would we want to be character-ized as a prisoner of anything, even hope?

Because being a prisoner of hope in God is dif-ferent. God's prisoners of hope aren't forced into an institution for punishment but invited into a fortress for safety. Imagine a castle that stands firm even when the very foundations of life are shaken. A place created just for us, where we can chain ourselves to the promise that God is work-ing all things for our good, even when all things are falling apart. From the high tower of this fortress, we prisoners of hope gain a whole new perspective. We can look beyond our unexpected circumstances to the future, trusting that God has good things in store for us.

When I first learned to think and live this

way, it was revolutionary to me. I was raised in a religious tradition that never encouraged me to expect good things from God. In fact, it was considered presumptuous to even imagine that God had time for my requests, given that he had an entire world to run. I'm so glad I discovered in his Word that God is good, God does good, and God wants to do good for me—all the time. But to keep my heart and mind thinking and believing this way on a daily basis doesn't come naturally; instead, it's always a choice, one I have to make again and again.

Here's another way to think about this choice. When the unexpected strikes, we find ourselves perched on a thin precipice with an abyss on either side. That's when we have a decision to make. We can choose to fall into the abyss of despair on one side or into the abyss of hope on the other. Both look like scary choices, but when we choose to fall into hope, we soon find ourselves wrapped in the arms of a loving God—a God who always catches us and always promises to carry us from the precipice of despair into the wide-open space of new life. That's where we find the new opportunities and experiences that get us beyond our disappointments and disillusionments. It is a place of freedom where we let go of what we once wanted in exchange for what we never expected—a new adventure. But we can't get there by ourselves. Only God can catch and carry us into the new life we never imagined and take us to places we never considered going.

Becoming a prisoner of hope doesn't mean we no longer struggle with disillusionment or despair. When the unexpected strikes and gives us new reasons to lose hope, it's still tempting to dig a tunnel out of our fortress, to escape hope and lose ourselves in doubt, fear, and unbelief. I cannot tell you how many times I almost lost hope that we would see people rescued at A21, or that traffickers would be caught and prosecuted and sentenced. That Propel Women would resonate with women. That I had another book in me. There were times I wondered if I would have the ability to parent my girls with wisdom. Or if I would get free from the pain of my past. The list is endless.

In each and every endeavor, I had to chain myself once more to the God of all hope. As we launched our initiatives, people left who had said they would stay. People who were supportive at one stage dropped out in the next. Doors slammed shut. Governments changed policies. But I have learned to walk by faith and not by sight.[10] To close my eyes, proclaim myself a prisoner of hope, and step into a spiritual fortress—to dare to get my hopes up and keep my hopes up. I've seen God step in and carry me to better places, present me with better opportunities, and lead me into amazing breakthroughs.

When we are tempted to escape but choose instead to run to our stronghold, Jesus, he promises to overflow our lives with hope: "Now may the

God of hope fill you with all joy and peace as you believe so that you may overflow with hope by the power of the Holy Spirit."[11]

He promises to help us become the prisoners of hope he's called us to be so we can move beyond despair into a new destiny.

But first, just as LoriAnn did, we have to willingly turn ourselves in at the fortress gate and stay there. When she said she knew God was a God of hope and that she had to press in and trust him, LoriAnn was making that choice. She was choosing to hope when there was no logical reason to hope and when everything around her was screaming at her to choose otherwise. LoriAnn's feelings of hopelessness were valid and painfully real, but by faith she chose to become a prisoner of hope, and, as strange as it sounds, that's where she found her true freedom. That's where she found her wide-open spaces—and it's where we will find ours.

I've had many unexpected things happen in

my life—things that were never in my plan. But in the same way LoriAnn's radiance and hope were a testimony to me, there is no telling what hope we can bring into our homes, workplaces, and communities if we'll choose to be people of hope—who use words of hope—in a world where people desperately need it. That's why LoriAnn had come to Greece to learn about A21—because she knew firsthand the power of hope to resurrect a life. She knew that as the people of God, we never have to lose hope, even in the most hopeless situations. She knew that the same Spirit that raised Jesus from the dead lived in her—and in every believer on earth—and that he has the power to resurrect new life from the ashes of suffering and pain. "If the Spirit of him who raised Jesus from the dead lives in you," wrote the apostle Paul, "then he who raised Christ from the dead will also bring your mortal bodies to life through his Spirit who lives in you."[12] That's a promise of hope that will not fail.

HOPE IS AN ACT OF DEFIANCE

I don't know where your hope is struggling. Maybe your beleaguered hope is for . . .

- A loved one to be saved.
- A child to come home.
- A marriage to be restored.
- Your body to be healed.
- Your finances to be restored.
- Your career to be revived.
- A home of your own.

Whatever it is, it's time to risk hoping again. Whatever dream we had that died, whatever promise we gave up on, the truth of God's Word says that we serve a God with resurrection power who specializes in raising the dead.[13] The truth we believe says we serve a God who redeems our lives from the pit, who gives us peace instead of conflict, who gives us a crown of beauty instead of ashes, who gives us the oil of joy instead of mourning, who gives us health instead of disease, liberty instead of captivity, assurance instead of doubt, hope instead of hopelessness.[14]

Our God is a transformational God. He transforms us from the inside out and makes all things new in our lives—first in our spirits when we accept him as our Lord and Savior, and then in our souls as we continue to surrender areas of our lives to him:

> Therefore, if anyone is in Christ, he is a new creation; the old has passed away, and see, the new has come! . . . He made the one who did not know sin to be sin for us, so that in him we might become the righteousness of God.[15]

God is a God of redemption, restoration, and new beginnings. He's made you a new creation, and that newness can work from the inside out to change your today into a better tomorrow. If you don't like where you are right now, you don't have to settle or resign yourself to it. You can hold onto his promise as the truth that triumphs over the facts in your life: "He who started a good work in you will carry it on to completion until the day of Christ Jesus."[16]

When we risk hoping again, we learn how to live in the present but with the future in mind. We shift the gaze of our focus forward. We become prisoners of hope who cling to hope, who speak the language of hope, who don't put off hope, who are willing to let God surprise us with a new future. When we become prisoners of hope, we commit a daring act of defiance—we dare to get our hopes up. We dare to believe that the desires God has placed in our hearts will be fulfilled—somehow and some way.[17]

Will they look like we first imagined? Probably not.

Will we go through more disappointments? Most likely.

Will any of our future dreams die as well before they come to life? Quite possibly.

Why? Because every promise is tested. Every dream is challenged. God does not always do what we want, when we want, or how we want—but he is always ready to do exceedingly, abundantly, above and beyond anything we could ever ask or think.[18] He who promised really is faithful, no matter what it looks like in any season of our lives. When we become prisoners of hope, we declare with defiance that there is . . .

- No need God cannot meet.
- No mountain God cannot move.
- No prayer God cannot answer.
- No sickness God cannot heal.
- No heart God cannot mend.
- No door God cannot open.

When we become prisoners of hope, we aren't dismayed when dreams . . .

- Take longer than we think they should.
- Cost more than we think they should.
- Are harder to realize than we think they should be.

When we become prisoners of hope, we shift our perspective. We . . .

- Look at what we have left, not what we have lost.
- Believe the best, not assume the worst.
- Keep moving forward, not shrinking backward.

It's time to become prisoners of hope, brave souls who are defiant in hope, who dare to get our hopes up. Let's refuse to throw away our confidence and trust in God, daring to believe he will reward our faith.

GOD RESTORES IN UNEXPECTED WAYS

When we risk becoming prisoners of hope, God can and will change what needs to be changed. We can get well. We can climb out of debt. We can forgive. We can be healed. We can overcome grief and loss—even the loss of a child. Losing a child at any stage of life is unimaginable pain and utterly devastating, and no child can ever be replaced, ever, but God can take us to a place where we no longer ache with our loss every moment of every day. If we lean into him, if we risk hoping and trusting him again, he can move us from our place of pain into a wide and spacious place of purpose. He can move us into a destiny we never might have considered. That's exactly what he did for LoriAnn.

Years after her miscarriages, God moved LoriAnn to a place where she became a mother to many. First, she became a stepmother to three children—including one she was blessed to mother from the time he was young. Next, she was invited to join the board of one of the largest child abuse prevention organizations in the United States and served in that role for years. And finally, she leads with Nick and me on the board of A21. God has made her maternal reach global—one in which her work benefits thousands upon thousands of children who have no mother to look after them. To her, that is the miracle God performed in her life, the double blessing Zechariah prophesied: "Return to your stronghold, O prisoners of hope; today I declare that I will restore to you double."[19]

"God healed my womb," LoriAnn once told me, "and I have become a mother to nations, something he put in my heart as a young girl."

Sometimes God gives us a revelation instead of a reason when he answers our prayers in unexpected ways. LoriAnn may never understand why she couldn't have her own children, but the call of God on her life to mother children still came to pass—and so did the fulfillment she longed for.

"He has used me because of my story," she said, "and not disqualified me because of what I have lived through." God is never finished with us—and whether we've gone through a divorce, a miscarriage, or suffered unimaginable hurts and losses in any area of our lives, he never sets us aside if we'll keep moving forward with him. If we'll keep putting our hope in him.

"But I had to learn a hard truth," LoriAnn added. "God fulfills what he puts in our hearts in unexpected ways. I had to learn that there are different ways I can mother. I can nurture and mentor young people. I can influence them and give them room in my heart. I can serve on boards that allow me to mother the motherless, to protect and shelter and defend the defenseless. It's so restorative to me to fight on behalf of women and children who can't fight for themselves. Isn't that what a mother does? A mother who wants the best for her children?"

Yes, it is.

God wants to fulfill the dreams he's whispered to our hearts—no matter how long ago. We may have set them aside, but he's never forgotten even one of them. Let's dare to open our hearts and minds and allow God to revive our hopes. Let's risk giving him room to fulfill his plans and purposes for our lives in unexpected ways.

WHAT YOU'VE LEARNED

* Hope is unshakeable confidence in God and a place of freedom where we let go of what we once wanted in exchange for what we never expected.

* God is good, God does good, and God wants to do good for us—all the time.

* Dare to get your hopes up and keep your hopes up.

QUESTIONS FOR
REFLECTION

Does it seem scary to become a "prisoner of hope"? If so, how can you move past that fear?

....

....

....

....

....

....

....

What dreams are you wanting to make a reality in your life? What are the first steps you can take to make those happen?

....

....

....

....

....

....

....

....

....

Life is full of the unexpected. What disappointments and discouragements, trials and traumas have you experienced in your life? Can you think of times when you later learned God had something good—perhaps even something better—waiting for you?

....

....

....

....

....

....

....

4

STEPS TOWARD HEALING
AND RESILIENCY

*Most people want to be circled by
safety, not by the unexpected. The
unexpected can take you out. But the
unexpected can also take you over
and change your life. Put a heart in
your body where a stone used to be.*

RON HALL

My friend Amanda had always been a strong person, certainly not someone given to hopelessness. But when the latest Mr. Right turned out to be all wrong, like all the others she'd dated, a cloud of disappointment threatened to overtake her in a way she'd never known. Like all of us, she felt like she could only take so much pain and disappointment before she hit a place of complete despair.

Maybe you've been there. Most of us don't grow up knowing how to process deep feelings of rejection in a healthy way, so we move through heartbreaking moments, piling up our pain and storing it in our hearts—until our hearts can't contain one more ounce of heartache. That's when we sometimes turn to coping in destructive ways. We simply want the pain to stop, and the feelings of hopelessness and despair to end.

That's what happened to Amanda. She grew up in a tiny southern US town of eight hundred people—the kind where everyone knows everyone and all their business. The kind where everyone attended church from the time they were babies. The kind where everyone grew up to marry a high school or college sweetheart. Everyone except Amanda.

That was when Amanda first remembers the hurt of disappointment trying to take up residence in her heart.

"Growing up, I remember always thinking, *I can't wait to be a wife!* I felt like God put that desire deep within me—and yet, I always had an awareness that it wouldn't happen in the normal way for me, whatever normal is. But I always trusted God. I knew I wanted to be married, and in our community, getting married was just as expected as breathing or going to school or work or church. It wasn't said aloud, but you weren't perceived as complete or to have even started your adult life until you were married.

"When my brother graduated from high school in May, he married in July. When my oldest sister graduated from high school in May, she married in June. When my next sister finished college—she married right after graduation. I went to college and graduated and was still single. I became the odd girl out."

As the years went by, Amanda kept trusting God, but being single grew into the heaviest burden she had ever known. And the repeated disappointments from failed relationships became as familiar as Sunday dinners.

"It was a mystery no one ever let you forget," Amanda said as she described year after year of being single. "Every family get-together included *the quiz*: 'Amanda, when are you going to get married? Have you met anyone lately? Maybe you are expecting too much in a man. Have you seen John's cousin Joe lately? He is really cute.'

"There was no dodging *the quiz*.

"My friends and family meant well. They loved

me, but they treated my singleness like a condition to cure. My heart wanted to be open to any and all good advice, but their suggestions chipped away at my confidence. When they suggested I was too intimidating, I would think, *What does that mean anyway? Why should I have to minimize who God created me to be so a man doesn't feel insecure around me? I don't want a guy I have to prop up by putting myself down.* They would suggest that I needed to try harder. *How do I 'try harder'?* They would say that I was too picky. That was always the hardest thing to hear. As much as I tried to be grateful for their concern, my heart felt like it was working overtime to stay positive. I did trust God, but walking it out every day in real life wasn't easy."

Amanda didn't date too many guys through the years, but she dated enough to know the chronic heartache when people—and life—fail us.

Her first serious boyfriend was also the first to break her heart. We'll call him Mr. Go-to-Jail:

"He was the first guy I opened my heart to. He came from a great family, fit in nicely with ours, but totally led a double life." Amanda winced. "So, he went to jail, and I went to college. I never could quite let my heart be fully open again until years later."

Then there was Mr. Gonna-Make-Money: "He was everything your mama wants you to bring home to meet the family," Amanda remembered. "He'd finished medical school and was starting his residency. He was financially stable. Charming. Successful. People in the church thought we were a darling couple—and the expectations grew. But over the months, I realized that he didn't want to pursue the Lord in the same way I did. It was so painful to leave the security of a man and to choose Jesus, but I knew I had to."

There was Mr. Let's-Just-Be-Friends: "I couldn't lie to myself," Amanda admitted. "I wanted our relationship to work so badly. I was so tired of the pressure of wanting to be married, of wanting to end all the feelings of the unknown, of always looking and wondering, of wanting to be seen and known and loved. I wanted to belong to someone. I wanted someone to hold me at the end of every day. But I knew he wasn't the one, so we parted ways as friends."

Eventually, there was the real Prince Charming, Mr. Too-Good-to-Be-True: Love. Romance. Thoughtfulness. Pursuit. Security. He seemed to provide it all. But it turned out to be a storybook romance without the storybook ending. The night they broke up was the final blow to her heart—the one that knocked all the life out of her.

That day was the culmination of almost a decade of dating that seemingly led nowhere. It was hard for Amanda to feel so successful in fulfilling her purpose, so fortunate in her friendships, but suffer one unexpected loss after another in dating. She had graduated from college, was consistently promoted in her work, was loved by everyone at her church, was adored by her family.

Definitely a viable catch. But when she couldn't make sense of why so many relationships unexpectedly failed, she plummeted emotionally. Even though she'd grown up in a great Christian home and served God in ministry for years, she had no idea how to manage the repeated disappointment. She had no idea how to refuse to allow the disappointment to cause her to retreat internally, shrink in her faith, and become fearful, unable to fully trust.

So, ten months after meeting Mr. Too-Good-to-Be-True, she sat on the couch drowning in disappointment that had a crippling effect—and the thoughts swirled, *What's wrong with me? Why am I always the odd girl out?*

STUCK IN A MOMENT

As the years go by and we wait for our dreams to come to pass, it takes courage to keep trusting

God, to keep our hearts open and tender, and to keep risking and trying again. At the beginning of any journey, it's easier to be full of zeal and keep a positive attitude. That's how Amanda started out with her desire to be a wife. She was full of expectant hope.

But then something happened. The first real boyfriend hurt her. And she withdrew, unable to completely open up again for the next few years.

Something similar happened to you—and me. Someone disappointed us. Something unexpected happened. Or, as in Amanda's life, the expected she had hoped for, longed for, lived for *didn't* happen. Either way, people—and life— failed us.

Disappointment happens to us all, in one way or another, because the Enemy will always make sure we get hit by at least a few blows that knock us off our feet with whatever dream we're pursuing. He's going to do whatever he can to stop our hopes for the best and to start our expectations for the worst. He's going to reinforce the belief that if we step out and risk our heart again, people will fail us again. And little by little, we move out of faith and into fear—and disappointments settle in our hearts and shrinks our dreams. And over time, that disappointment leads us to doubt and pull back. We withdraw to protect ourselves from ever risking hurt again.

We grow numb.

We stop trusting in God's promise to us—or doubt that we ever heard it in the first place. We stop dreaming new dreams—or stop fueling the ones we once held dear.

Disappointment—that let-down feeling where our emotions bottom out and our faith does too—is a powerful, destructive force. It can leave us stuck in a painful moment through which we filter and even forfeit future experiences. It is a force we have to face and overcome to live a life full of faith embracing the unexpected and all that God has for us.

MANAGING DISAPPOINTMENT

When life doesn't go our way—which it rarely does—and when our expectations lead to utter disappointment, we don't always know how to recover our trust of God. When disappointments happen repeatedly, our hearts can grow sick, and our thoughts can grow dark. That's when the Enemy can move in and steal the last of our hope. That's when doubt and unbelief can overtake what's left of our faith.

But disappointment is inevitable throughout life because we all have expectations, whether big or small, and sometimes those expectations don't get met:

- Friends break their word.
- Our marriage ends.
- A colleague betrays us.
- Our kids disappoint us.
- We never have the child we long for.

- We never find our soulmate.
- We don't get the promotion.
- We lose our retirement fund.
- A dream turns into a nightmare.
- We disappoint ourselves by saying or doing something we regret.

But despite what we experience and how we feel, all the disappointment in the world will never change the promises of God, the reality of Jesus, or his destiny for our lives. None of our broken dreams, personal heartaches, or shattered plans can stop his desire for us to fulfill our purpose. The disappointment is real. The consequences can be devastating. To keep moving forward, we must learn to be resilient. We must learn to trust and risk trusting again. We must learn to manage our disappointments well so we can go again full of renewed hope. Otherwise, while we're stuck in the disappointment behind us, we'll miss the adventure God is setting before us.

I don't know why I had a miscarriage between having my two girls, but I trust him.

I don't know why women, children, and men are trafficked all over the world, but I trust him—and I choose to be part of the solution.

I don't know why I wasn't miraculously and instantly healed of cancer, but I am thankful for all I went *through* to be well.

I don't know what has broken down along the way in your life. I don't know why your life has experienced unexpected events, but will you join me in trusting God once again?

What one experience has stopped you in your tracks?

What one experience has shaken you to your core and stolen all your confidence?

What one experience have you believed disqualifies you for the purpose to which God called you?

Do you see how it's what we *do* with our disappointments that determines our destiny? If we don't go *through* our hardships, we may move on in years, but our life stops at the point of our greatest disappointment. We either go *through* what happens and manage the disappointments well, or they manage us.

Has it ever occurred to you that if you'll revisit your disappointment, God can give you a new perspective on it—one that can become a tool for your own healing and to help others heal? That you can take what he gives to you and pass it on? This is the very principle the apostle Paul describes in his second letter to the church at Corinth:

> Blessed be the God and Father of our Lord Jesus Christ, the Father of mercies and the God of all comfort. He comforts us in all our affliction, so that we may be able to comfort those who are in any kind of affliction, through the comfort we ourselves receive from God.[1]

Has it ever occurred to you that God can use your disappointments to set a new trajectory for you, one that gets you closer to your destiny? That's something I've experienced over and over again. All the disappointments in my life have ultimately become tools I could use to serve others. I will not let the Enemy get the last word, because I believe there are divine appointments beyond all our disappointments.

Trusting God is a series of choices, not a one-time event. It's the process of growth the apostle Paul described as working out our salvation.

"Therefore, my dear friends, just as you have always obeyed, so now, not only in my presence but even more in my absence, work out your own salvation with fear and trembling. For it is God who is working in you both to will and to work according to his good purpose."[2] Trusting God requires something of us, which is why Paul calls it "work." It means choosing again and again and again to:

- Stay connected to God and his process. Daily.
- Process disorientation through God's perspective. Immediately.
- Risk, be vulnerable, and believe. Resiliently.
- Ask God for help when we don't have the answers. Courageously.

Choosing to trust God is part of how we live an intentional life. We choose not to avoid disappointment. Not to avoid pain. But rather to learn to manage our disappointments well and to embrace the truth that the new adventure ahead holds, even when it looks differently than we expected.

Disappointment is a place we're meant to pass through, not a place where we're meant to stay. God wants us emotionally engaged in his purposes. Living in the moment. Fully alive. Hopeful. He wants us to let him restore our hearts so we can keep moving forward and fulfill his good purpose for our lives. Even when people—and life—fail us.

God wants us to be resilient. The American Psychological Association (APA) defines resilience as "the process and outcome of successfully adapting to difficult or challenging life experiences" like adversity, trauma, tragedy, threats, or significant sources of stress.[3] According to one source, "Personal resilience is an ongoing, lifelong learning process." There's also "community resilience," which is "the sustained ability of a community to utilize available resources to respond to, withstand, and recover from adverse situations." Then there is "radical resilience," which "integrates social and healing justice into this work by recognizing and addressing historical institutional barriers and systems of oppression." This approach involves self- and collective care.[4]

Being radically resilient is an approach more than it is a mindset. I would suggest that it allows us to trust God and invite him in to care for us and bring healing into our lives. Being resilient helps us give our bodies, minds, and spirits the space to heal and persevere.

RECOVER YOUR WONDER

God wants us to believe and understand that his promises don't have expiration dates. They aren't like passports or gym memberships. They aren't like the condiments in the fridge or the food in the pantry. Our heavenly Father has given us a book full of his promises that have no expiration dates—and he will always make good on his promises.

Holding to our faith—even in the face of deep disappointment—is critical. Making God's promises bigger than our disappointments is essential. Getting into his Word and letting it get into us brings our hearts back to life. Worshiping him opens the door for the Holy Spirit to encourage us and heal us so we can trust again. Learning how to change our perspective through steps like these helps us transition from fearing the unexpected to trusting God through it.

Do we trust that God is who he says he is?

Do we trust that God will do what he says he will do?

Do we trust that God is working all things together for our good and his glory?

Do we trust that "he who promised is faithful?"[5]

Until we change our perspective, we won't see things clearly, and we'll even miss God ministering directly to us—much like the two disciples who walked together in sorrow along the road to Emmaus.

The two disciples, who were leaving Jerusalem heartbroken and bitterly disappointed, had followed Jesus and trusted him, only to be shocked and disillusioned by his crucifixion. All their hope had been in Jesus and how he was the one to redeem Israel. But their dreams had died on the cross with Jesus.

Now that same day two of them were going to a village called Emmaus, about seven miles from Jerusalem. They were talking with each other about everything that had happened. As they talked and discussed these things with each other, *Jesus himself came up and walked along with them; but they were kept from recognizing him.*

He asked them, "What are you discussing together as you walk along?"

They stood still, *their faces downcast.* One of them, named Cleopas, asked him, *"Are you the only one visiting Jerusalem who does not know the things that have happened there in these days?"*

"What things?" he asked.

"About Jesus of Nazareth," they replied. "He was a prophet, powerful in word and deed before God and all the people. The chief priests and our rulers handed him over to be sentenced to death, and they crucified him; but we had hoped that he was the one who was going to redeem Israel. And what is more, it is the third day since all this took place. In addition, some of our women amazed us. They went to the tomb early this morning but didn't find his body. They came and told us that they had seen a vision of angels, who said he was alive. Then some of our companions went to the tomb and found it just as the women had said, but they did not see Jesus."

He said to them, "How foolish you are, and how slow to believe all that the prophets have spoken! *Did not the Messiah have to suffer these things and then enter his glory?" And beginning with Moses and all the Prophets, he explained to them what was said in all the Scriptures concerning himself.*

As they approached the village to which they were going, Jesus continued on as if he were going farther. But they urged him strongly, "Stay with us, for it is nearly evening; the day is almost over." So he went in to stay with them.

When he was at the table with them, he took bread, gave thanks, broke it and began to give it to them. *Then their eyes were opened and they recognized him, and he disappeared from their sight.* They asked each other, "Were not our hearts burning within us while he talked with us on the road and opened the Scriptures to us?"

They got up and returned at once to Jerusalem. There they found the Eleven and those with them, assembled together and saying, "It is true! The Lord has risen and has appeared to Simon." Then the two told what had happened on the way, and how Jesus was recognized by them when he broke the bread.[6]

These disciples had been with Jesus the week before his crucifixion and were full of hope. But when he was crucified, they lost all hope and headed to Emmaus. Their world came apart because the events did not unfold as they had anticipated. Even with all the rumors of the resurrection, they still did not believe Jesus was alive.

Their journey through disappointment and disillusionment to renewed hope is often the same path we follow:

- *Jesus began talking to them, but they could not recognize his voice.*[7] How many times does he speak to our hearts, yet we're so lost in our own concerns that we cannot hear him?

- *Their eyes were downcast.*[8] They were crushed and couldn't even look up to see the fellow traveler walking alongside them. As long as we look down at our circumstances, and not up at him, we'll miss what it is that we need to see—what he wants us to see.

- *They asked the only one who really knew what had happened if he had any idea of the disappointing events.*[9] When we finally ask God what he thinks, we open the door for the clarity only he can bring.

- *He brought them back to the Word.*[10] Jesus knew the promises of God and explained how those promises would be fulfilled in a way that would change the world. He told them that a new kingdom was at hand. It is always the Word that changes our perspective from disappointment to hope.

- *Finally, they saw him in the midst of their disappointment.*[11] How powerful it is when we can look up and see God, even when our circumstances are ongoing.

- *They got up at once. Their wonder came back.*[12] When our hope is renewed, we are strengthened to move forward.

Jesus always walks with us through our disappointment. Through our heartaches. Leading us to recover our wonder. Leading us to something better ahead. Leading us to dream again. He is the one who helps us remember that although the unexpected happened to us, he'll never leave us.

Jesus has been there for me in every unexpected disappointment.

And he is there for you right now, wherever you are.

WHAT YOU'VE LEARNED

* When we get stuck in disappointment, we have to get unstuck. It's a place we move through, not a destination.

* It's what we do with our disappointments that determines our destiny.

* We must be resilient and hold on to our faith even in the midst of our disappointments.

QUESTIONS FOR REFLECTION

What's one experience you've had that has shaken your spiritual foundations? How did you move forward?

....

....

....

....

....

....

Can you think of times in your life when God's promises have proven to be true for you?

Resilience gives us the space to heal and persevere. When you're going through a difficult time, what are specific ways you can support your body, mind, and spirit in order to cultivate that space?

5

TIMING

There is a time for everything,
and a season for every activity
under the heavens.
ECCLESIASTES 3:1 (NIV)

*R*eady is a tricky word when it comes to following Jesus and doing his will. Why? Because there is a huge difference between feeling ready and actually being ready.

Did Moses feel ready to return to Egypt and tell Pharaoh to let his people go? No. It seemed an impossible mission.

Did Gideon feel ready to go strike down the Midianites and save Israel? No.

Did Jeremiah feel ready to be a prophet to the nations? No.

Did young Mary, a virgin teenager, feel ready to carry the Son of God in her womb? No.

God's Word records the accounts of their questions, protests, reservations, and pleas demonstrating that they didn't feel ready.[1]

In fact, we can go through the Bible page by

page and find person after person who didn't *feel* ready to do what God called them to do. But God didn't ask them whether they *felt* ready. He decided they *were* ready. Then he called them and told them what to do. Those we now call heroes of the faith are the ones who obeyed God's call even when they did not feel ready.

God knew he had prepared them. He knew he would provide whatever they needed. He knew what he was going to accomplish through them even though his plans seemed impossible by human standards. So he called them and sent them. We can be certain of this: when God calls us and sends us, we are ready, whether we feel we are or not.

How ready are you?

Don't misunderstand. Everyone has an entirely different calling. You may be called to care for an aging parent or to steer a troubled teen through a tumultuous time or to lead your family through a financial crisis. You may see the need to organize a local food pantry. Perhaps a neighbor is caught in an abusive relationship and needs your help, or a spouse is suffering from depression, or the local elementary school has appealed for after-school mentors for children who have no one at home to read to them or help them with their homework. Maybe you've become increasingly aware, during your daily commute, of the people experiencing homelessness on the streets of your city, or you feel an inner nudge to volunteer for the youth ministry at your church. Or maybe you went to visit a loved one in prison and saw the loneliness and hopelessness of those who had no visitors.

Perhaps there is a pressing social issue you feel that your company, or your church, should be addressing. Do you sense a growing desire to invest less of your time in the career you've been developing for decades and more of your time in compassionate work with those who don't even have a job, much less a career?

The point is: God's call comes to each of us in

every age and stage of life. He calls us to step out of our comfort zone and into our race, ready to run for him and carry the love of God and the truth of his power into the lives of others. Often, we have no idea what task the Lord will assign to us until it is thrust into our hands.

WHAT HOLDS YOU BACK?

Because our God is God of the impossible, the seemingly impossible can't hold us back from achieving God's purposes for us. But other things can. Failure to enter the race or an unwillingness to take a route God shows us will keep us from the thrill of playing our part. It's time to throw out our excuses.

Allow me to ask a personal question: What's holding you back?

Here is why I ask. I travel the globe talking with Christians in every walk of life and every phase of Christian maturity, and I've discovered that our churches are filled with brothers and sisters who, for a host of reasons, feel dissatisfied with their spiritual condition.

- Some are new believers just beginning to understand the nature, character, and purposes of God. They are eager to run but not sure how to get started.
- Others attend church but are weary or burned out from living a busy or self-focused Christian life without seeing the life change or the world change they long for.
- Some have lost interest in attending church and feel the established church has lost its relevance, but they themselves long to be relevant in the world, to make a difference.
- Most long for a taste of God's power and presence unlike anything they've ever known.
- Many believe they are not qualified or gifted enough to be used by God in big ways.

Did you find yourself in this list? If I missed aptly describing your current spiritual condition, but you too feel that something is missing in your spiritual life, take a few minutes to articulate the problem.

Once you've identified where you are, here's the good news: God has an eternal purpose for the whole body of Christ and a divinely chosen part for every single believer. He has uniquely designed and selected each and every believer to fulfill his or her purpose. I'm going to repeat that, because it's that important.

God has an eternal purpose for the whole body of Christ and a divinely chosen part for every single believer. He has uniquely designed and selected each and every believer to fulfill his or her purpose.

That includes you, my friend. If you seek God's will, if you offer yourself to run his race, then he will equip you to join or return to the race, no matter how impossible that may seem. Not only will he equip you as an individual runner for personal spiritual enrichment, but he will also train you as part of the team, the church of Jesus Christ. We have been entrusted with the mission of advancing the kingdom of God on the earth. Never underestimate how huge, how mighty, how world-changing and eternity-altering this race really is.

When you step forward, willing to join the race and run, you will see that the seemingly impossible—your making a difference in this world—isn't impossible at all. God has empowered you with his very own Holy Spirit to run to win.

When Nick and I started A21 more than fifteen years ago, I had no idea where it would take me. I did not realize how many legs to this race there were. I keep handing off more and more with every new office that opens and every gathering I address; and now, so many others are running with us. The surprise of this divine race is that just when you think you've finished one leg of the race, you discover that the best part is still ahead, that

God has so much more in mind for you than you ever imagined. The ride is so wild and thrilling that the more I run, the more my passion grows to run even more.

THE MULTIPLICATION FACTOR

When we run with God into all he's called us to do, when we move forward in obedience, God multiplies our efforts. This divine multiplication factor is critically important for us to understand. Why? Because all too often, rather than seeing ourselves as qualified by God to play a great part in his race, we look at our lives—our limitations, our meager resources, our brokenness, our apparent insignificance in this huge world—and rather than moving forward into his plans and purposes for us, we feel unqualified to be used mightily by God, and so we slink to the sidelines.

But the race isn't run from the sidelines! The

Christian life is no spectator sport. It is heartbreaking for me to meet Christians who love the Lord and desire to serve him but who shy away from playing their part because they don't understand God's divine multiplication factor. How tempting to look at our broken world and messy lives and falsely believe we are too broken, the pain is too much, the evil of this world is too entrenched for us to make a difference. Countless believers are stopped dead in their tracks before they get started. "After all," they reason, "I'm just one person. My involvement isn't going to make a dent in what's wrong in this world. I'm not qualified enough for God to use me in important ways."

Of course we are small, but God is huge.

Of course we have limitations, but God is limitless.

Of course we are weak, but God is strong.

Of course we are finite, but God is infinite.

Of course we are imperfect, but God is perfect.

Of course we fail, but God never fails.

Of course we can choose to stop, but God is unstoppable.

And if we choose to move forward with every dream he drops in our hearts, with everything he's called us to do, with everything our calling entails, he gladly multiplies our efforts and makes us and our impact on this world greater.

God calls you to run your race not because you are mighty and strong. He calls you to take your place in the race because he is mighty and strong, and he plans to accomplish his work in you and through you!

HOW NOT ENOUGH BECOMES MORE THAN ENOUGH

Some two thousand years ago, on a hillside swarming with thousands of hungry people, the disciples found themselves confronted with a problem that looked too big to overcome. Watch what unfolded as God multiplied what was offered to him. And look for how God speaks to you about running your race.

Jesus had been teaching and healing a large crowd all day.[2] His words were so life-giving, so earth-shattering, that the people stayed hour after hour after hour to hear more. Late in the day, the disciples came to Jesus, saying he should send the people away so they could go to surrounding villages and buy themselves something to eat.

So Jesus asks, "How many loaves do you have?"

Andrew, one of the disciples, comes back with, "Here is a boy with five small barley loaves and two small fish, but how far will they go among so many?" Notice that Andrew didn't just say it was five barley loaves and two fish. He called them *small* loaves and *small* fish, as if he wanted to emphasize that such a small amount was insignificant in light of the huge need.

Notice that Jesus asks them how much there is to go around. He makes sure that the disciples recognize the limitations they are facing. Often it is when we come face-to-face with our limitations that we give up, thinking all is lost. But when we recognize our limitations, then we also recognize when God demonstrates his limitless power. Until we hit our limit, we often assume we can provide, we can deliver, and we can produce.

What are you facing today that brings you face-to-face with your limitations, leaving you questioning how qualified you are to make a difference in this broken world? Is it a broken past? A dream that has died? A lack of time, money, education, leadership skills, influence, or confidence? We must never assess a difficulty in light of our own resources but in light of God's resources. You can step boldly into all that God has for you to do not because you have no limits (we all have plenty!) but because *God's resources are limitless.* Jesus accepted the five loaves and two fish, small though they were. One packed lunch. A meager amount of food. It was all the boy had, but he offered it all. If the boy had kept his little lunch, then it would have remained little. If you keep your little, then it will remain little as well. But if you step into God's plans and purposes for your life, what little you have will be multiplied.

When the boy gave his little to Jesus, Jesus blessed it, and it became much in Jesus' hands. It is never about how little we have. It is about what our little has the potential to become in the hands of a miracle-working God. Don't focus on what you don't have, what you can't do, what isn't enough. Just offer your "not enough" to God, and he will multiply it into *more* than enough. That's what happens when you are running your race, offering yourself to be used by God.

I love this next part! Do you know the first thing Jesus did with that meager offering? He looked up to heaven and gave thanks to God for the little he was given by the boy. I wonder what it was like for that boy to see his meager meal held up to the heavens by the hands of a grateful Jesus.

Jesus, of course, knew it wasn't going to remain little, that it was about to be multiplied into great abundance. But let's not miss this moment: the Son of God, holding our offering up to Almighty God and blessing it with his thanks! We don't need to know *how* God is going to use our meager offering. We only need to know that he *wants* to use it. Always remember that *God celebrates our gifts to him and blesses them.*

Next, Jesus broke the bread and the fish. When he blessed it, there were five and two. But when he broke it, we lose count. The more Jesus broke the bread and fish, the more there was to feed and nourish. The disciples started distributing the food, and soon what was broken was feeding thousands. The miracle is in the breaking. It is in the breaking that God multiplies not enough into more than enough.

Are there broken places in your life so painful that you fear the breaking will destroy you? Are there broken places from past years? Are there relationships that feel broken beyond repair? With your spouse, children, or extended family? Friends or coworkers? Have you experienced brokenness in your body? Or in your mind? Have your dreams, plans, education, career paths, or finances been broken?

You may be thinking that your brokenness has disqualified you from being able to run in the race, but as with my own life, when we give God our brokenness, it qualifies us to be used by God to carry hope, restoration, and grace to others on the sidelines who too have been broken.

Put your broken pieces into God's hands and watch him use them to work his wonders. Some of the most life-giving people I have met have gone through something that broke them and allowed them to see God use for his glory that which the Enemy meant for evil. *When our broken pieces are offered to God, he multiplies them for his purposes.*

Not only was there enough for everyone to

have their fill, there were leftovers! Listen to what Jesus said when everyone had been filled and satisfied: "He said to his disciples, 'Gather the pieces that are left over. Let nothing be wasted.'"[3]

Did you hear Jesus' words? *"Let nothing be wasted."* So precious to the Lord are our offerings, our broken pieces, that even when he's multiplied them into an overabundance, he puts every bit of it to good use. The next time you are tempted to withhold your contribution to the kingdom, believing it to be too small or too broken to make a difference, don't forget that not only will God celebrate, bless, and multiply your contribution, he will also value every little bit of it. *God never wastes what we offer to him.*

All four of the disciples who wrote the Gospels—Matthew, Mark, Luke, and John—record this miraculous hillside feeding, and all report the number of people fed as five thousand men, which did not include the women and children. Matthew 14:21 made that very clear: "Now those who ate were about five thousand men, besides women and children."

Have you ever noticed that part of the verse? I used to think, *Why didn't they count everybody? Why only the men?* until a powerful realization occurred to me.

Whose lunch was it that Jesus multiplied? It was a child who gave his meager lunch—an *uncounted* boy! The disciples did not count the very one who God had moved into position to release his miracle.

Isn't that just like God to use people who other people do not count?

You may think you are too insignificant to count, but God counts you. In fact, he more than counts you. God counts *on* you. *The uncounted count.* You matter.

Are you holding back from stepping boldly into the next leg of your race because you feel that you have nothing extraordinary to offer? God is not waiting for you, hoping you'll eventually bring him extraordinary talents, abilities, accomplishments, and gifts. The time is now to give him what you have, no matter how ordinary or insignificant it may seem. In his divine race, *God uses the ordinary to do the extraordinary.*

WHAT YOU'VE LEARNED

* When God calls us and sends us, we are ready, whether we feel we are or not.

* Each of us has a unique purpose in God's plan.

* Not only will God celebrate, bless, and multiply your contribution, he will also value every little bit of it.

QUESTIONS FOR REFLECTION

What's holding you back from running your unique race? What limitations or worries do you have that keep you from going all in?

Can you think of a time when you—even as "just one person"—were able to make a difference?

As we saw in the feeding of the five thousand, the miracle is in the breaking. How have you seen broken places in your life transformed into *more*?

....

....

....

....

....

....

....

....

....

....

6

REMEMBERING YOUR WHY AND SAYING YES

"Faith is taking the first step even when you can't see the whole staircase."
MARTIN LUTHER KING, JR.

God places in our hearts a calling, a mission, a goal, an idea, a destiny, and then he leads us to it through small, incremental steps. It's a principle of growth depicted throughout the Bible. The prophet Isaiah said it this way: "He tells us everything over and over—one line at a time, one line at a time, a little here, and a little there!"[1] This same step-by-step process is evident in how God led the children of Israel out of slavery in Egypt and into the promised land. They had been enslaved for 430 years, and God knew they had an enslaved mentality that would hold them back from possessing all God had for them. As much as they wanted to leave Egypt and get quickly to the promised land, God didn't race them across the desert. Instead, he led them on an unexpected journey through the desert.

I deeply resonate with this story. Even though God put a desire in my heart to serve him when I first became a believer, I was not ready *then* for all the initiatives I lead *now*. He had to begin healing me by renewing my mind from an enslaved mentality—from a victim who had been abandoned, adopted, and abused—so I could step into whatever promised land he had for me in my future.

Likewise, even though God freed the children of Israel and led them to the promised land, he couldn't let them possess all the land immediately. Instead, he worked a very deliberate plan—one that I believe he works in our lives as well. When he marched them across the Jordan River, they faced all the inhabitants living in the land, including the giants Caleb eventually defeated. But God didn't lead them to conquer all the inhabitants in a short period of time—rather, he helped his people to drive them out little by little:

I will not drive them out ahead of you in a single year; otherwise, the land would become desolate, and wild animals would multiply against you. I will drive them out *little by little* ahead of you until you have become numerous and take possession of the land.[2]

God's directive displayed his infinite wisdom and vision for their future. While they were tired and weary of waiting and wanting to rush right in, God knew they couldn't yet manage all that real estate. He knew that in their current condition, the land they desperately wanted—the land he had promised them—had the power to destroy them. So, he showed them how to achieve their mutual goal little by little. They needed to grow stronger first, so he put them on a strength training plan. In the process, he prepared the land for them and prepared them for the land.

Can you relate at all to the mindset of the

ancient Israelites? Have you ever wanted to rush headlong into whatever it was you felt called by God to do? If so, welcome to the club! Most of us want our destiny on demand. We want all of God's promises to be *yes* and *amen* and *now*. But that's not how God's little-by-little method works. God is process-oriented. Consider just a few other areas of life where we see this principle very clearly. Little by little, we:

- Lose weight and build muscle.
- Get debt-free by discipline and delayed gratification.
- Acquire our education and qualifications.
- Build trust in relationships.
- Write books.

And the list could go on. Virtually everything in our human experience is accomplished little by little. That's how God works—little by little.

STEP BY STEP

In God's little-by-little process, steps are essential for success, whether it's in our personal life, professional life, or spiritual and emotional development. When I started traveling through New South Wales' small towns, speaking in high schools, and inviting students to nighttime rallies, I was taking steps. I was building on what I'd learned working with youth at church and in the youth center. Those first two steps prepared me for my work with Youth Alive, a church-sponsored nationwide youth organization. And that third step, which lasted seven years, prepared me for the next steps. But it all began with the first step:

- I went to church.
- I said yes to serving at a cleanup day.
- I said yes to volunteering at the youth center.

- I said yes to serving as the New South Wales director of Youth Alive.
- I said yes to starting Equip & Empower Ministries.
- I said yes to initiating A21.
- I said yes to launching Propel Women, and then Propel Ecclesia, a coaching and cohort experience for women in ministry.

It's not that one thing led directly to the next thing; it's that one *step* led to the next *step*—and I couldn't bypass any of the steps. It was like climbing a set of stairs, and what I learned on each step gave me the wisdom, knowledge, strength, confidence, and maturity to succeed when I moved up to the next one.

Here is an example of just one way that happened. When I worked for the youth center in Sydney, before I went to serve with Youth Alive in the countryside, I started meeting with government advisors to discuss youth policies. I went to school after school conducting seminars and working with the faculty to develop after-school programs and to write curriculum. How could I have known then that someday, through the work of A21, we would develop a curriculum that is now distributed throughout schools in the United States? How could I have known that God would use my early years of writing and developing a local curriculum to produce a far more extensive one?

God knew the end from the beginning, but I did not.

God knew he was preparing me, but I did not.

God knew all the unexpected moments were leading somewhere. I just trusted him and took steps, and *he has never wasted one step.* "The LORD directs the steps of the godly," wrote the psalmist. "He delights in every detail of their lives."[3] There are no express elevators to our destination, because God does not take elevators—he directs our steps. And if we're growing, little by little he shows us just one next step at a time.

I know it's not always easy. Trusting him for the next step has sometimes been deeply painful and difficult for me. So many times, I wanted to skip steps, but I've seen people do that, and it always leads to a much more painful process. If we skip a step, then we will still have to learn what was involved in that step—but chances are we'll have to learn it at a higher cost and in a more public way. Personally, I'd rather learn *everything* I can on each step—every bit of revelation and understanding—so I don't get knocked down by the events of life ahead. I want the image of Christ to be fully formed in me. I want the nine fruits of the Spirit[4] fully developed in me—love, joy, peace, patience, kindness, goodness, faithfulness, gentleness, and self-control. I want to walk in mature love, because that is what I want to flow out of me to a lost and broken world. We simply cannot despise small beginnings[5]—or small steps.

Steps keep us dependent on God. They keep us on our knees in prayer, walking by faith and not by sight.[6] It's human nature to want to know the whole story first—to see the whole staircase from bottom to top—but we can't possibly know the end from the beginning. I certainly didn't.

THE COURAGE TO TRUST

Often, when things get worse before they get better, harder before easier, darker before lighter, we doubt. We doubt our dreams. We doubt God. We doubt his calling. We doubt his faithfulness. We give up. *I guess he didn't open that door. I guess he didn't call me. I guess this isn't his will.* When did God say that it would be easy? When did he say it would be effortless?

Here are a few things I have learned over and over and over again while following God:

- Closed doors do not mean that God is not opening a way.

- Increased cost does not mean that God is not calling.
- The presence of a battle does not mean the absence of God in the war.

Trials don't mean we are out of the will of God. In fact, they often mean we are precisely in the center of God's will—right where we're supposed to be, doing exactly what we're supposed to be doing. Fighting the good fight of faith. Standing. Believing. Because he is working in all things for our good.[7]

In the beginning years of A21, as Nick and I and our team kept taking steps of faith, we often ran into unexpected roadblocks. It felt like we were constantly being rerouted, something I find to be a common experience in the Christian life. When we say yes to God—to the dreams and ideas he places in our hearts—the roads are often winding, uphill, uncharted, and full of potholes. They frequently require unexpected detours, the kind that don't show up on any map. And sometimes it seems like it takes much longer to get there than we ever expected. So it was when we launched A21 in Greece.

Many times, it would have made much more sense to give up, but God was at work positioning us and preparing us. And eight years later, as the global refugee crisis unfolded in 2015—a historic event with a once-in-a-lifetime opportunity to help people—God showed us just how faithful he is, especially when we don't give up. When multiple humanitarian organizations were not allowed to respond, we were. The Greek government only would allow "established" agencies to help. Because we had been operational since 2008, we were considered established and thereby qualified to help.

Sometimes it seems far more logical to give up than to keep having faith for something to happen. The dream or promise God has placed in your heart probably isn't logical. You may not have the resources. You may not know much about the mission. You may not even know where to begin.

Or your dream may be more personal. You want to see someone you love saved or healed. Whatever the dream or the promise, God keeps his promises—and whether or not it happens as we expect really doesn't matter.

Very little in my life has ever happened the way I thought it would—but God's plans have prevailed because I've never stopped believing in him and following what he has wanted me to do. I've learned over and over that he often does unexpected things in unexpected ways in unexpected places using unexpected people.

People like you and me.

For Nick and me, starting an organization that covered everything from *reach* (prevention measures that increase global awareness) to *rescue* (assisting with law enforcement rescuing human trafficking victims) to *restoration* (aftercare for survivors) was not logical. No one was doing all that then. But that didn't matter. God seems to rarely ask us to do something in which we have expertise or a template. He wants us to rely on him, trust him, and stay connected to him—for as long as it takes. Whatever dream God has placed in our hearts to believe, to long for, to plan, to build is never something to give up on.

So, what has God placed in your heart to do? What has he called you to do that you have yet to start?

There will always be opportunities to falter, to slow down, to give up. But there is an assignment carved out for you, and God wants you to fulfill it.

God has certainly not forgotten what it is. If he said it, he will do it. If he tells you to do something, he will help you accomplish it. It may take what *feels* like a lifetime, but *he will do it*. And the results will most likely be very unexpected. And by unexpected, I mean wildly better than you could hope or imagine.

WHAT YOU'VE LEARNED

* God knows the end from the beginning, but we do not.

* Being constantly rerouted is a common experience in the Christian life.

* God always keeps his promises—but often in unexpected ways.

QUESTIONS FOR REFLECTION

When have you doubted God's plan or promises in your life? Are there current doubts you're experiencing?

....

....

....

....

....

....

....

Have you ever felt the desire to jump head-long into God's calling for you or to skip steps along the way?

....

....

....

....

....

....

....

....

....

What dream has God placed in your heart to do? What "little by little" steps can you start taking today?

....

....

....

....

....

....

....

....

....

....

PRAYING THE SCRIPTURES

I don't know what you have prayed for, believed for, longed for, cried for, but the facts of your present never negate the truth of God's promise for your future—no matter how much time has passed. God's promises don't have expiration dates. If he promised it, then it will happen.

Our part is to be flexible and receptive to how he wants to fulfill the promise, because, most likely, the fulfillment will look different than we expect. And we can't confuse due dates with due seasons. We aren't promised due dates—specific times we might hold on to—but we are promised due seasons—God's perfect timing: "And let us not grow weary while doing good, for in due season we shall reap, if we do not lose heart" (Galatians 6:9, NKJV).

If you have prayed about something God has

called you to do, commissioned you to accomplish, compelled you to complete, then persevere in faith, believing no matter what. If you have grown weary, risk trusting God again and start judging God as faithful to do what he promised (Hebrews 10:23). Our prayers are effective and meaningful to God. He is good, he does good, and he is working all things together for our good—even when things don't look good (Romans 8:28). He is moving whether or not we see progress.

I have always prayed, whether or not things unfolded as I expected. And truthfully, nothing—and I mean nothing—in my life has gone as I expected. But it has all worked out. Thus far, everything God has wanted to accomplish through me has somehow come to pass. It didn't look like I thought it would. It didn't happen in the timing I thought it would. It didn't come from the resources I thought it would. It didn't come because of the people I thought it would. But it did happen—eventually. Due season did come. That's why I believe we can pray and trust God in the face of the impossible.

If you've pulled back, it's time to lean in, to move toward hope and trust. God answers prayers; he answers our prayers. And to help you pray according to his will, according to his Word, I've included key scriptures from each chapter. Take each one and personalize it, boldly going to God's throne with it and putting him in remembrance of his Word (Isaiah 43:26).

If you are unsure how to do this, consider the following verse from Psalm 32:8: "I will instruct you and show you the way to go; with my eye on you, I will give counsel."

This is a promise we can personalize in prayer: Heavenly Father, please instruct me with your counsel today and show me the way to go as you have promised in your Word. I'm so grateful you have your eye on me. I trust you to help me. In Jesus' name, amen.

With faith and trust in God, nothing is impossible.

CHAPTER 1

SEE WHAT GOD SEES AND LOOK TO YOUR FUTURE

"God decided in advance to adopt us into his own family by bringing us to himself through Jesus Christ. This is what he wanted to do, and it gave him great pleasure." EPHESIANS 1:5 NLT

"Love consists in this: not that we loved God, but that he loved us and sent his Son to be the atoning sacrifice for our sins." 1 JOHN 4:10

"Do not remember the past events; pay no attention to things of old. Look, I am about to do something new; even now it is coming." ISAIAH 43:18–19

"Commit your way to the Lord; trust in him, and he will act." PSALM 37:5

"I am certain that God, who began the good work within you, will continue his work until it is finally finished on the day when Christ Jesus returns." PHILIPPIANS 1:6 NLT

"Many are the plans in the mind of a man, but it is the purpose of the Lord that will stand." PROVERBS 19:21 ESV

"Trust in the Lord with all your heart, and do not rely on your own understanding; in all your ways know him, and he will make your paths straight." PROVERBS 3:5–6

"The thief comes only to steal and kill and destroy; I have come that they may have life, and have it to the full." JOHN 10:10 NIV

"Let all bitterness, anger and wrath, shouting and slander be removed from you, along with all malice. And be kind and compassionate to one another, forgiving one another, just as God also forgave you in Christ." EPHESIANS 4:31–32

"Therefore, as God's chosen ones, holy and dearly loved, put on compassion, kindness, humility, gentleness, and patience, bearing with one another and forgiving one another if anyone has a grievance against another. Just as the Lord has forgiven you, so you are also to forgive." COLOSSIANS 3:12–13

CHAPTER 2
ACKNOWLEDGE YOUR FUTURE AND REMOVE THE SHAME

"But you will receive power when the Holy Spirit has come on you, and you will be my witnesses in

Jerusalem, in all Judea and Samaria, and to the ends of the earth." ACTS 1:8

"God has not given us a spirit of fear, but one of power, love, and sound judgment." 2 TIMOTHY 1:7

"The Lord is the Spirit, and where the Spirit of the Lord is, there is freedom." 2 CORINTHIANS 3:17

"But now you are free from the power of sin and have become slaves of God. Now you do those things that lead to holiness and result in eternal life." ROMANS 6:22 NLT

"If you look carefully into the perfect law that sets you free, and if you do what it says and don't forget what you heard, then God will bless you for doing it." JAMES 1:25 NLT

"Jesus said to the Jews who had believed him, 'If you continue in my word, you really are my disciples. You will know the truth, and the truth will set you free.'" JOHN 8:31–32

"For freedom, Christ set us free. Stand firm, then, and don't submit again to a yoke of slavery." GALATIANS 5:1

"Love the Lord your God with all your heart, with all your soul, and with all your strength." DEUTERONOMY 6:5

"Be wholeheartedly devoted to the Lord our God to walk in his statutes and to keep his commands, as it is today." 1 KINGS 8:61

"He himself bore our sins in his body on the tree; so that, having died to sins, we might live for righteousness. By his wounds you have been healed." 1 PETER 2:24

CHAPTER 3

ACCEPTING DISAPPOINTMENT
AND REMAINING HOPEFUL

"The LORD *is near the brokenhearted; he saves those crushed in spirit."* PSALM 34:18

"My flesh and my heart may fail, but God is the strength of my heart, my portion forever." PSALM 73:26

"Come to me, all of you who are weary and burdened, and I will give you rest. Take up my yoke upon you and learn from me, because I am lowly and humble in heart, and you will find rest for your souls." MATTHEW 11:28–29

"For no one is cast off by the Lord forever. Though he brings grief, he will show compassion, so great is his unfailing love. For he does not willingly bring affliction or grief to anyone." LAMENTATIONS 3:31–33 NIV

"When you pass through the waters, I will be with you, and the rivers will not overwhelm you. When you walk through the fire, you will not be scorched, and the flame will not burn you." ISAIAH 43:2

"Yet I call this to mind, and therefore I have hope: Because of the Lord's faithful love we do not perish, for his mercies never end. They are new every morning; great is your faithfulness!" LAMENTATIONS 3:21–23

"May your faithful love rest on us, LORD, for we put our hope in you." PSALM 33:22

"For nothing will be impossible with God."
LUKE 1:37

"There is surely a future hope for you, and your hope will not be cut off." PROVERBS 23:18 NIV

"How long will I store up anxious concerns within me, agony in my mind every day? How long will my enemy dominate me? Consider me and answer, Lord my God. Restore brightness to my eyes; otherwise, I will sleep in death. My enemy will say, 'I have triumphed over him,' and my foes will rejoice because I am shaken. But I have trusted in your faithful love; my heart will rejoice in your deliverance. I will sing to the Lord because he has treated me generously."
PSALM 13:2–6

CHAPTER 4

STEPS TOWARD
HEALING AND RESILIENCY

"Be sober-minded, be alert. Your adversary the devil is prowling around like a roaring lion, looking for anyone he can devour. Resist him, firm in the faith, knowing that the same kind of sufferings are being experienced by your fellow believers throughout the world." 1 PETER 5:8–9

"Put on the full armor of God so that you can stand against the schemes of the devil." EPHESIANS 6:11

"Therefore, my dear brothers and sisters, be steadfast, immovable, always excelling in the Lord's work, because you know that your labor in the Lord is not in vain." 1 CORINTHIANS 15:58

"We are afflicted in every way but not crushed; we are perplexed but not in despair; we are persecuted but not abandoned; we are struck down but not destroyed." 2 CORINTHIANS 4:8–9

"I have told you these things so that in me you may have peace. You will have suffering in this world. Be courageous! I have conquered the world." JOHN 16:33

"Lord my God, I cried to you for help, and you healed me." PSALM 30:2

"Rejoice in hope; be patient in affliction; be persistent in prayer." ROMANS 12:12

"The Lord is my strength and my shield; my heart trusts in him, and I am helped. Therefore my heart celebrates, and I give thanks to him with my song." PSALM 28:7

"Do not fear, for I am with you; do not be afraid, for I am your God. I will strengthen you; I will help you; I will hold on to you with my righteous right hand." ISAIAH 41:10

"Jesus said to her, 'I am the resurrection and the life. The one who believes in me, even if he dies, will live. Everyone who lives and believes in me will never die.'" JOHN 11:25–26

CHAPTER 5

TIMING

"The Lord will fulfill his purpose for me. Lord, your faithful love endures forever." PSALM 138:8

"You are a chosen people, a royal priesthood, a holy nation, God's special possession, that you may declare the praises of him who called you out of darkness into his wonderful light." 1 PETER 2:9 NIV

"We are his workmanship, created in Christ Jesus for good works, which God prepared ahead of time for us to do." EPHESIANS 2:10

"He said to me, 'My grace is sufficient for you, for my power is perfected in weakness.' Therefore, I will most gladly boast all the more about my weaknesses, so that Christ's power may reside in me." 2 CORINTHIANS 12:9

"Then Job answered the Lord and said: 'I know that you can do all things, and that no purpose of yours can be thwarted.'" JOB 42:1–2 ESV

"[Jesus] replied, 'What is impossible with man is possible with God.'" LUKE 18:27

"Just as a branch is unable to produce fruit by itself unless it remains on the vine, neither can you unless you remain in me. I am the vine; you are the branches. The one who remains in me and

I in him produces much fruit, because you can do nothing without me." JOHN 15:4–5

"My God will supply all your needs according to his riches in glory in Christ Jesus."
PHILIPPIANS 4:19

"[God] said to me, 'Behold, I will make you fruitful and multiply you, and I will make of you a company of peoples and will give this land to your offspring after you for an everlasting possession.'"
GENESIS 48:4 ESV

"She said, 'As the Lord your God lives, I don't have anything baked—only a handful of flour in the jar and a bit of oil in the jug. Just now, I am gathering a couple of sticks in order to go prepare it for myself and my son so we can eat it and die.'

Then Elijah said to her, 'Don't be afraid; go and do as you have said. But first make me a small loaf from it and bring it out to me.

Afterward, you may make some for yourself and your son, for this is what the Lord God of Israel says, "The flour jar will not become empty and the oil jug will not run dry until the day the Lord sends rain on the surface of the land."'

So she proceeded to do according to the word of Elijah. Then the woman, Elijah, and her household ate for many days. The flour jar did not become empty, and the oil jug did not run dry, according to the word of the Lord he had spoken through Elijah." 1 KINGS 17:12–16

CHAPTER 6
REMEMBERING YOUR WHY AND SAYING YES

"I am God, and no one is like me. I declare the end from the beginning, and from long ago what is not yet done, saying: my plan will take place, and I will do all my will." ISAIAH 46:9–10

"Jesus Christ is the same yesterday, today, and forever." HEBREWS 13:8

"Do not be conformed to this age, but be transformed by the renewing of your mind, so that you may discern what is the good, pleasing, and perfect will of God." ROMANS 12:2

"The Lord your God will drive out these nations before you little by little. You will not be able to destroy them all at once; otherwise, the wild animals will become too numerous for you." DEUTERONOMY 7:22

"Then I heard the voice of the Lord asking: Who will I send? Who will go for us? I said: Here I am. Send me." ISAIAH 6:8

"Those who know your name trust in you because you have not abandoned those who seek you, Lord." PSALM 9:10

"*Blessed is the one who endures trials, because when he has stood the test he will receive the crown of life that God has promised to those who love him.*" JAMES 1:12

"*The person who trusts in the Lord, whose confidence indeed is the Lord, is blessed. He will be like a tree planted by water: it sends its roots out toward a stream, it doesn't fear when heat comes, and its foliage remains green. It will not worry in a year of drought or cease producing fruit.*" JEREMIAH 17:7–8

"*Indeed, God is my salvation; I will trust him and not be afraid, for the Lord, the Lord himself, is my strength and my song. He has become my salvation.*" ISAIAH 12:2

"*Now faith is the assurance of things hoped for, the conviction of things not seen. For by it the people of old received their commendation.*"
HEBREWS 11:1–2 ESV

NOTES

INTRODUCTION

1. John 17:18.

1. SEE WHAT GOD SEES AND LOOK TO YOUR FUTURE

1. Gen. 50:20 (NIV).
2. 1 Cor. 9:24–25.
3. Heb. 12:1.
4. Eph. 3:20 (NKJV).

2. ACKNOWLEDGE YOUR FUTURE AND REMOVE THE SHAME

1. Jer. 29:11.
2. Phil. 3:7–8.
3. Phil. 3:13–14 (NIV).
4. Jer. 29:11.
5. Acts 3:1–10.

6. *Lexham Bible Dictionary.*

7. John D. Barry et al., *Lexham Bible Dictionary* (Lexham Press, 2016).

8. Acts 3:11–26; Acts 4:4.

3. ACCEPTING DISAPPOINTMENT AND REMAINING HOPEFUL

1. James 4:8.

2. John 14:6.

3. Matt. 5:4; 2 Cor. 1:3–5.

4. Zech. 9:12 (ESV).

5. Shane J. Lopez and C.R. Snyder, eds. "Memoriam: Remembering C.R. Snyder: A Humble Legacy of Hope," *The Oxford Handbook of Positive Psychology*, 2nd ed. (2009; online ed., Oxford Academic, September 18, 2012), https://academic.oup.com/edited-volume/28153/chapter/212928489, accessed August 8, 2023.

6. Rachel Colla et al., "'A New Hope' for Positive Psychology: A Dynamic Systems

Reconceptualization of Hope Theory,"
Frontiers in Psychology 13:809053 (2022), doi:
10.3389/fpsyg.2022.809053.

7. Mind Tools Content Team, "Snyder's Hope
Theory," *Mind Tools*, www.mindtools.com/
aov3izj/snyders-hope-theory.

8. Heb. 10:35.

9. Ps. 39:7.

10. 2 Cor. 5:7.

11. Rom. 15:13.

12. Rom. 8:11.

13. Matt. 9:24.

14. Isa. 61:3; Ps. 103.

15. 2 Cor. 5:17, 21.

16. Phil. 1:6.

17. Psalm 37:4.

18. Eph. 3:20–21.

19. Zech. 9:12 (ESV).

4. STEPS TOWARD HEALING AND RESILIENCY

1. 2 Cor. 1:3–4.

2. Phil. 2:12–13

3. American Psychological Association, *APA Dictionary of Psychology*, s.v. "resilience," https://dictionary.apa.org/resilience.

4. UCSC Healthy Campus, "Radical Resilience," https://healthycampus.ucsc.edu/wellness-initiatives/radical-resilience.

5. Heb. 10:23.

6. Luke 24:13–35 (NIV); emphasis added.

7. Luke 24:17.

8. Luke 24:17.

9. Luke 24:18.

10. Luke 24:25–27.

11. Luke 24:31.

12. Luke 24:33.

5. TIMING

1. Moses' initial protests to God's call are recorded in Exodus 3:6–4:14. Gideon's doubts and protests are found in Judges 6. Jeremiah's feelings of inadequacy and the Lord's

response to them are found in Jeremiah 1:4–10. Mary, perplexed at how she, a virgin, could give birth to the Son of God, was humbled and willing, as recorded in Luke 1:26–55.

2. Mark 6:30–44; Luke 9:10–17; Matt. 14:13–21; John 6:1–15.
3. John 6:12 (NIV).

6. REMEMBERING YOUR WHY AND SAYING YES

1. Isa. 28:10 (NLT).
2. Ex. 23:29–30; emphasis added.
3. Ps. 37:23 (NLT).
4. Gal. 5:22–23.
5. Zech. 4:10.
6. 2 Cor. 5:7.
7. 1 Tim. 6:12; Eph. 6:13; Rom. 8:28.

In this year-long planner format, Christine shows us the life-changing power of living in the moment while looking toward the future.

Available wherever books are sold.